THE GOSPEL ACCORDING TO
ST. MATTHEW

TODAY'S ENGLISH VERSION ✣

CHRIST IN MAJESTY WITH SYMBOLS OF THE EVANGELISTS

The Gospel According To
St. Matthew

Today's English Version

American Bible Society
New York

The Gospel According to Matthew

Imprimatur:
✠Most Reverend William H. Keeler, D. D.
President, National Conference of
Catholic Bishops

March 10, 1993

This is a Portion of Holy Scripture in the *Today's English Version* from the Good News Bible. The American Bible Society is a not-for-profit organization which publishes the Scriptures without doctrinal note or comment. Since 1816, its single mission has been to make the Word of God easily available to people everywhere at the lowest possible cost and in the languages they understand best. Working toward this goal, the ABS is a member of the United Bible Societies, a worldwide effort that extends to more than 200 countries and territories. You are urged to read the Bible and to share it with others. For a free catalog of other Scripture publications, call the American Bible Society at 1-800-32-BIBLE, or write to 1865 Broadway, New York, NY 10023-7505. Visit the ABS website! **www.americanbible.org**

Front cover art: St. Matthew the Evangelist, Scala/Art Resource, NY

Frontispiece: The British Library

ISBN 1-58516-184-5

Printed in the United States of America
Eng. Port. TEV560P-109883
ABS-8/00-3,000—CG1

FOREWORD

The Good News Bible in *Today's English Version* is a new translation which seeks to state clearly and accurately the meaning of the original texts in words and forms that are widely accepted by people who use English as a means of communication. This translation does not follow the traditional vocabulary and style found in the historic English Bible versions. Rather it attempts in this century to set forth the biblical content and message in the standard, everyday, natural form of English.

The aim of this Bible is to give today's reader maximum understanding of the content of the original texts. The preface explains the nature of special aids for readers which are included in the volume. It also sets forth the basic principles which translators followed in their work.

The Bible in *Today's English Version* was translated and published by the United Bible Societies for use throughout the world. The Bible Societies trust that the reading and study of this translation will result in a better understanding of the meaning of the Bible. We also earnestly pray that readers will discover the message of saving faith and hope for all people which the Bible contains.

Introduction to the Gospels

The Gospels provide various pictures of the life and teachings of Jesus Christ. The word "Gospel" comes from an Old English word that means "good news." The Greek word that is translated as "gospel" or "good news" is *euangelion* (see MARK 1.1). The English words "evangelist" and "evangelism" come from this word. An evangelist is one who tells good news.

The Gospels (Matthew, Mark, Luke, and John) were probably written down in their present form between 30 and 60 years after Jesus died and was raised to life by God. Since Jesus himself left no writings, the Gospels record stories and eyewitness descriptions that had been passed on by word of mouth for a number of years. At first, Jesus' followers were so eager to tell the message about him that they didn't think it was necessary to write down what he had said and done. But as Jesus' first followers and eyewitnesses grew older and died, it became more important to have a written record of Jesus and his teachings, and to describe his death and how God brought him back to life.

Although other "gospels" were written, the only ones accepted as reliable by the whole church were MATTHEW, MARK, LUKE, and JOHN. It is not certain who actually wrote the Gospels, since the names of the authors are never given in the books that bear the names of MATTHEW, MARK, LUKE, and JOHN. The Gospels were probably written between A.D. 60, ten years before the temple was destroyed in Jerusalem, and A.D.100. Most scholars agree that MARK was most likely the first Gospel written, since MATTHEW and LUKE seem to take many of their details and the order of events directly from MARK.

Many sources were used to create the Gospels. These probably included various collections of Jesus' sayings and stories that were available to the Gospel writers. For example, a number of Jesus' sayings are similar in MATTHEW and LUKE, so they may have been working with the same source. They also appear to have used MARK for their basic outlines. But MATTHEW and LUKE used different sources to describe the events surrounding Jesus' birth, since MARK begins after Jesus is already grown up. Because MATTHEW, MARK, and LUKE have so much material in common and follow the same basic outline, they are sometimes referred to as the "Synoptic" Gospels (from the Greek word synopsis, which means "seeing together").

These Synoptic Gospels are more like each other than any of them is like the Gospel of JOHN. While MATTHEW, MARK, and LUKE focus on Jesus' public teaching and miracle working in Galilee, JOHN contains information about Jesus' early work in Judea. These include the so-called "I am" sayings, such as "I am the bread that gives life!" (JOHN 6.35); "I am the light for the world!" (John 8.12); and many more. The order of events in JOHN does not follow the order shared by MATTHEW, MARK, and LUKE. And JOHN does not include any of Jesus' stories (parables) that are found in the other three Gospels. Each Gospel presents its own perspective on the events of Jesus' life and his teachings. For more about what makes each of these accounts of Jesus' life and ministry unique, see the Introduction to each Gospel.

The Gospel according to
MATTHEW

INTRODUCTION

The Gospel according to Matthew tells the good news that Jesus is the promised Savior, the one through whom God fulfilled the promises he made to his people in the Old Testament. This good news is not only for the Jewish people, among whom Jesus was born and lived, but for the whole world.

Matthew is carefully arranged. It begins with the birth of Jesus, describes his baptism and temptation, and then takes up his ministry of preaching, teaching, and healing in Galilee. After this the Gospel records Jesus' journey from Galilee to Jerusalem and the events of Jesus' last week, culminating in his crucifixion and resurrection.

This Gospel presents Jesus as the great Teacher, who has the authority to interpret the Law of God, and who teaches about the Kingdom of God. Much of his teaching is gathered by subject matter into five collections: (1) the Sermon on the Mount, which concerns the character, duties, privileges, and destiny of the citizens of the Kingdom of heaven (chapters 5–7); (2) instructions to the twelve disciples for their mission (chapter 10); (3) parables about the Kingdom of heaven (chapter 13); (4) teaching on the meaning of discipleship (chapter 18); and (5) teaching about the end of the present age and the coming of the Kingdom of God (chapters 24–25).

OUTLINE OF CONTENTS

The Ancestors of Jesus Christ
(Luke 3.23-38)

1 This is the list of the ancestors of Jesus Christ, a descendant of David, who was a descendant of Abraham.

2-6a From Abraham to King David, the following ancestors are listed: Abraham, Isaac, Jacob, Judah and his brothers; then Perez and Zerah (their mother was Tamar), Hezron, Ram, Amminadab, Nahshon, Salmon, Boaz (his mother was Rahab), Obed (his mother was Ruth), Jesse, and King David.

6b-11 From David to the time when the people of Israel were taken into exile in Babylon, the following ancestors are listed: David, Solomon (his mother was

1.11 2 K 24.14, 15; 2 Ch 36.10; Jr 27.20

the woman who had been Uriah's wife), Rehoboam, Abijah, Asa, Jehoshaphat, Jehoram, Uzziah, Jotham, Ahaz, Hezekiah, Manasseh, Amon, Josiah, and Jehoiachin and his brothers.

¹²⁻¹⁶ From the time after the exile in Babylon to the birth of Jesus, the following ancestors are listed: Jehoiachin, Shealtiel, Zerubbabel, Abiud, Eliakim, Azor, Zadok, Achim, Eliud, Eleazar, Matthan, Jacob, and Joseph, who married Mary, the mother of Jesus, who was called the Messiah.

¹⁷ So then, there were fourteen generations from Abraham to David, and fourteen from David to the exile in Babylon, and fourteen from then to the birth of the Messiah.

The Birth of Jesus Christ
(Luke 2.1-7)

¹⁸ This was how the birth of Jesus Christ took place. His mother Mary was engaged to Joseph, but before they were married, she found out that she was going to have a baby by the Holy Spirit. ¹⁹ Joseph was a man who always did what was right, but he did not want to disgrace Mary publicly; so he made plans to break the engagement privately. ²⁰ While he was thinking about this, an angel of the Lord appeared to him in a dream and said, "Joseph, descendant of David, do not be afraid to take Mary to be your wife. For it is by the Holy Spirit that she has conceived. ²¹ She will have a son, and you will name him Jesus — because he will save his people from their sins."

²² Now all this happened in order to make come true what the Lord had said through the prophet, ²³ "A virgin will become pregnant and have a son, and he will be called Immanuel" (which means, "God is with us").

²⁴ So when Joseph woke up, he married Mary, as the angel of the Lord had told him to. ²⁵ But he had no sexual relations with her before she gave birth to her son. And Joseph named him Jesus.

Visitors from the East

2 Jesus was born in the town of Bethlehem in Judea, during the time when Herod was king. Soon afterward, some men who studied the stars came from the East to Jerusalem ² and asked, "Where is the baby born to be the king of the Jews? We saw his star when it came up in the east, and we have come to worship him."

³ When King Herod heard about this, he was very upset, and so was everyone else in Jerusalem. ⁴ He called together all the chief priests and the teachers of the Law and asked them, "Where will the Messiah be born?"

⁵ "In the town of Bethlehem in Judea," they answered. "For this is what the prophet wrote:
⁶ 'Bethlehem in the land of Judah,
　you are by no means the least
　　of the leading cities of
　　　Judah;
for from you will come a leader
　who will guide my people
　　Israel.' "

⁷ So Herod called the visitors from the East to a secret meeting and found out from them the exact time the star had appeared. ⁸ Then he sent them to Bethlehem with these instructions: "Go and make a careful search for the child; and when you find him, let me know, so that I too may go and worship him."

⁹⁻¹⁰ And so they left, and on their way they saw the same star they had seen in the East. When they saw it, how happy they were, what joy was theirs! It went ahead of them until it stopped over the place where the child was. ¹¹ They went into the house, and when they saw the child with his mother Mary, they knelt down and worshiped him. They brought out their gifts of gold, frankin-

---

1.18 Lk 1.27　**1.21** Lk 1.31　**1.23** Is 7.14 (LXX)　**1.25** Lk 2.21　**2.6** Mic 5.2

The star . . . went ahead of them. (2.9-10)

cense, and myrrh, and presented them to him.

¹²Then they returned to their country by another road, since God had warned them in a dream not to go back to Herod.

The Escape to Egypt

¹³After they had left, an angel of the Lord appeared in a dream to Joseph and said, "Herod will be looking for the child in order to kill him. So get up, take the child and his mother and escape to Egypt, and stay there until I tell you to leave."

¹⁴Joseph got up, took the child and his mother, and left during the night for Egypt, ¹⁵where he stayed until Herod died. This was done to make come true what the Lord had said through the prophet, "I called my Son out of Egypt."

The Killing of the Children

¹⁶When Herod realized that the visitors from the East had tricked him, he was furious. He gave orders to kill all the boys in Bethlehem and its neighborhood who were two years old and younger — this was done in accordance with what he had learned from the visitors about the time when the star had appeared.

¹⁷In this way what the prophet Jeremiah had said came true:
¹⁸"A sound is heard in Ramah,
    the sound of bitter weeping.
Rachel is crying for her children;
    she refuses to be comforted,
    for they are dead."

The Return from Egypt

¹⁹After Herod died, an angel of the Lord appeared in a dream to Joseph in Egypt ²⁰and said, "Get up, take the child and his mother, and go back to the land of Israel, because those who tried to kill the child are dead." ²¹So Joseph got up, took the child and his mother, and went back to Israel.

²²But when Joseph heard that Archelaus had succeeded his father Herod as king of Judea, he was afraid to go there. He was given more instructions in a dream, so he went to the province of Galilee ²³and made his home in a town named Nazareth. And so what the prophets had said came true: "He will be called a Nazarene."

The Preaching of John the Baptist
(Mark 1.1-8; Luke 3.1-18; John 1.19-28)

3 At that time John the Baptist came to the desert of Judea and started preaching. ²"Turn away from your sins," he said, "because the Kingdom of heaven is near!" ³John was the man the prophet Isaiah was talking about when he said,

    "Someone is shouting in the
        desert,
      'Prepare a road for the Lord;
      make a straight path for him
        to travel!' "

⁴John's clothes were made of camel's hair; he wore a leather belt around his waist, and his food was locusts and wild honey. ⁵People came to him from Jerusalem, from the whole province of Judea, and from all over the country near

2.15 Ho 11.1   2.18 Jr 31.15   2.23 Mk 1.24; Lk 2.39; Jn 1.45   3.2 Mt 4.17; Mk 1.15
3.3 Is 40.3 (LXX)   3.4 2 K 1.8

the Jordan River. ⁶They confessed their sins, and he baptized them in the Jordan.

⁷When John saw many Pharisees and Sadducees coming to him to be baptized, he said to them, "You snakes — who told you that you could escape from the punishment God is about to send? ⁸Do those things that will show that you have turned from your sins. ⁹And don't think you can escape punishment by saying that Abraham is your ancestor. I tell you that God can take these rocks and make descendants for Abraham! ¹⁰The ax is ready to cut down the trees at the roots; every tree that does not bear good fruit will be cut down and thrown in the fire. ¹¹I baptize you with water to show that you have repented, but the one who will come after me will baptize you with the Holy Spirit and fire. He is much greater than I am; and I am not good enough even to carry his sandals. ¹²He has his winnowing shovel with him to thresh out all the grain. He will gather his wheat into his barn, but he will burn the chaff in a fire that never goes out."

The Baptism of Jesus
(Mark 1.9-11; Luke 3.21, 22)

¹³At that time Jesus arrived from Galilee and came to John at the Jordan to be baptized by him. ¹⁴But John tried to make him change his mind. "I ought to be baptized by you," John said, "and yet you have come to me!"

¹⁵But Jesus answered him, "Let it be so for now. For in this way we shall do all that God requires." So John agreed.

¹⁶As soon as Jesus was baptized, he came up out of the water. Then heaven was opened to him, and he saw the Spirit of God coming down like a dove and lighting on him. ¹⁷Then a voice said from heaven, "This is my own dear Son, with whom I am pleased."

The Temptation of Jesus
(Mark 1.12, 13; Luke 4.1-13)

4 Then the Spirit led Jesus into the desert to be tempted by the Devil. ²After spending forty days and nights without food, Jesus was hungry. ³Then the Devil came to him and said, "If you are God's Son, order these stones to turn into bread."

"Order these stones to turn into bread!" (4.3)

⁴But Jesus answered, "The scripture says, 'Human beings cannot live on bread alone, but need every word that God speaks.'"

⁵Then the Devil took Jesus to Jerusalem, the Holy City, set him on the highest point of the Temple, ⁶and said to him, "If you are God's Son, throw yourself down, for the scripture says,

'God will give orders to his
     angels about you;
   they will hold you up with
     their hands,
   so that not even your feet will
     be hurt on the stones.'"

⁷Jesus answered, "But the scripture also says, 'Do not put the Lord your God to the test.'"

3.7 Mt 12.34; 23.33   **3.9** Jn 8.33   **3.10** Mt 7.19   **3.17** Gn 22.2; Ps 2.7; Is 42.1; Mt 12.18; 17.5; Mk 1.11; Lk 9.35   **4.1** He 2.18; 4.15   **4.4** Dt 8.3 **4.6** Ps 91.11, 12   **4.7** Dt 6.16

⁸Then the Devil took Jesus to a very high mountain and showed him all the kingdoms of the world in all their greatness. ⁹"All this I will give you," the Devil said, "if you kneel down and worship me." ¹⁰Then Jesus answered, "Go away, Satan! The scripture says, 'Worship the Lord your God and serve only him!'" ¹¹Then the Devil left Jesus; and angels came and helped him.

Jesus Begins His Work in Galilee
(Mark 1.14, 15; Luke 4.14, 15)

¹²When Jesus heard that John had been put in prison, he went away to Galilee. ¹³He did not stay in Nazareth, but went to live in Capernaum, a town by Lake Galilee, in the territory of Zebulun and Naphtali. ¹⁴This was done to make come true what the prophet Isaiah had said,
¹⁵"Land of Zebulun and land of
   Naphtali,
on the road to the sea, on the
   other side of the Jordan,
Galilee, land of the Gentiles!
¹⁶The people who live in darkness
   will see a great light.
On those who live in the dark
   land of death
   the light will shine."
¹⁷From that time Jesus began to preach his message: "Turn away from your sins, because the Kingdom of heaven is near!"

Jesus Calls Four Fishermen
(Mark 1.16-20; Luke 5.1-11)

¹⁸As Jesus walked along the shore of Lake Galilee, he saw two brothers who were fishermen, Simon (called Peter) and his brother Andrew, catching fish in the lake with a net. ¹⁹Jesus said to them, "Come with me, and I will teach you to catch people." ²⁰At once they left their nets and went with him.

²¹He went on and saw two other brothers, James and John, the sons of Zebedee. They were in their boat with their father Zebedee, getting their nets ready. Jesus called them, ²²and at once they left the boat and their father, and went with him.

Jesus Teaches, Preaches, and Heals
(Luke 6.17-19)

²³Jesus went all over Galilee, teaching in the synagogues, preaching the Good News about the Kingdom, and healing people who had all kinds of disease and sickness. ²⁴The news about him spread through the whole country of Syria, so that people brought to him all those who were sick, suffering from all kinds of diseases and disorders: people with demons, and epileptics, and paralytics — and Jesus healed them all. ²⁵Large crowds followed him from Galilee and the Ten Towns, from Jerusalem, Judea, and the land on the other side of the Jordan.

The Sermon on the Mount

5 Jesus saw the crowds and went up a hill, where he sat down. His disciples gathered around him, ²and he began to teach them:

True Happiness
(Luke 6.20-23)

³"Happy are those who know they
   are spiritually poor;
the Kingdom of heaven
   belongs to them!
⁴"Happy are those who mourn;
   God will comfort them!
⁵"Happy are those who are
   humble;
they will receive what God
   has promised!

4.10 Dt 6.13   4.12 Mt 14.3; Mk 6.17; Lk 3.19, 20   4.13 Jn 2.12   4.15, 16 Is 9.1, 2
4.17 Mt 3.2   4.23 Mt 9.35; Mk 1.39   5.4 Is 61.2   5.5 Ps 37.11

6"Happy are those whose greatest
    desire is to do what
    God requires;
    God will satisfy them fully!
7"Happy are those who are
    merciful to others;
    God will be merciful to them!
8"Happy are the pure in heart;
    they will see God!
9"Happy are those who work for
    peace;
    God will call them his
    children!
10"Happy are those who are
    persecuted because they
    do what God requires;
    the Kingdom of heaven
    belongs to them!
11"Happy are you when people insult
you and persecute you and tell all kinds
of evil lies against you because you are
my followers. 12Be happy and glad, for
a great reward is kept for you in heaven.
This is how the prophets who lived before you were persecuted.

Salt and Light
(Mark 9.50; Luke 14.34, 35)

13"You are like salt for the whole
human race. But if salt loses its salti-
ness, there is no way to make it salty
again. It has become worthless, so it is
thrown out and people trample on it.
14"You are like light for the whole
world. A city built on a hill cannot be
hid. 15No one lights a lamp and puts it
under a bowl; instead it is put on the
lampstand, where it gives light for
everyone in the house. 16In the same
way your light must shine before people, so that they will see the good things
you do and praise your Father in
heaven.

Teaching about the Law

17"Do not think that I have come to
do away with the Law of Moses and the
teachings of the prophets. I have not
come to do away with them, but to
make their teachings come true. 18Re-
member that as long as heaven and
earth last, not the least point nor the
smallest detail of the Law will be done
away with — not until the end of all
things.ª 19So then, whoever disobeys
even the least important of the commandments and teaches others to do
the same, will be least in the Kingdom
of heaven. On the other hand, whoever
obeys the Law and teaches others to do
the same, will be great in the Kingdom
of heaven. 20I tell you, then, that you
will be able to enter the Kingdom of
heaven only if you are more faithful
than the teachers of the Law and the
Pharisees in doing what God requires.

Teaching about Anger

21"You have heard that people were
told in the past, 'Do not commit murder; anyone who does will be brought to
trial.' 22But now I tell you: if you are an-
gryᵇ with your brother you will be
brought to trial, if you call your brother
'You good-for-nothing!' you will be
brought before the Council, and if
you call your brother a worthless fool
you will be in danger of going to the fire
of hell. 23So if you are about to offer
your gift to God at the altar and there
you remember that your brother has
something against you, 24leave your
gift there in front of the altar, go at once
and make peace with your brother,
and then come back and offer your
gift to God.
25"If someone brings a lawsuit
against you and takes you to court, set-

ª the end of all things; or all its teachings come true.   ᵇ if you are angry; some
manuscripts have if without cause you are angry.
5.6 Is 55.1, 2   **5.8** Ps 24.3, 4   **5.10** 1 P 3.14   **5.11** 1 P 4.14
5.12 2 Ch 36.16; Ac 7.52   **5.13** Mk 9.50; Lk 14.34, 35   **5.14** Jn 8.12; 9.5
5.15 Mk 4.21; Lk 8.16; 11.33   **5.16** 1 P 2.12   **5.18** Lk 16.17   **5.21** Ex 20.13; Dt 5.17

tle the dispute while there is time, before you get to court. Once you are there, you will be turned over to the judge, who will hand you over to the police, and you will be put in jail. ²⁶There you will stay, I tell you, until you pay the last penny of your fine.

Teaching about Adultery

²⁷"You have heard that it was said, 'Do not commit adultery.' ²⁸But now I tell you: anyone who looks at a woman and wants to possess her is guilty of committing adultery with her in his heart. ²⁹So if your right eye causes you to sin, take it out and throw it away! It is much better for you to lose a part of your body than to have your whole body thrown into hell. ³⁰If your right hand causes you to sin, cut it off and throw it away! It is much better for you to lose one of your limbs than to have your whole body go off to hell.

Teaching about Divorce
(Matthew 19.9; Mark 10.11, 12; Luke 16.18)

³¹"It was also said, 'Anyone who divorces his wife must give her a written notice of divorce.' ³²But now I tell you: if a man divorces his wife for any cause other than her unfaithfulness, then he is guilty of making her commit adultery if she marries again; and the man who marries her commits adultery also.

Teaching about Vows

³³"You have also heard that people were told in the past, 'Do not break your promise, but do what you have vowed to the Lord to do.' ³⁴But now I tell you: do not use any vow when you make a promise. Do not swear by heaven, for it is God's throne; ³⁵nor by earth, for it is

the resting place for his feet; nor by Jerusalem, for it is the city of the great King. ³⁶Do not even swear by your head, because you cannot make a single hair white or black. ³⁷Just say 'Yes' or 'No'—anything else you say comes from the Evil One.

Teaching about Revenge
(Luke 6.29, 30)

³⁸"You have heard that it was said, 'An eye for an eye, and a tooth for a tooth.' ³⁹But now I tell you: do not take revenge on someone who wrongs you. If anyone slaps you on the right cheek, let him slap your left cheek too. ⁴⁰And if someone takes you to court to sue you for your shirt, let him have your coat as well. ⁴¹And if one of the occupation troops forces you to carry his pack one mile, carry it two miles. ⁴²When someone asks you for something, give it to him; when someone wants to borrow something, lend it to him.

Love for Enemies
(Luke 6.27, 28, 32-36)

⁴³"You have heard that it was said, 'Love your friends, hate your enemies.' ⁴⁴But now I tell you: love your enemies and pray for those who persecute you, ⁴⁵so that you may become the children of your Father in heaven. For he makes his sun to shine on bad and good people alike, and gives rain to those who do good and to those who do evil. ⁴⁶Why should God reward you if you love only the people who love you? Even the tax collectors do that! ⁴⁷And if you speak only to your friends, have you done anything out of the ordinary? Even the pagans do that! ⁴⁸You must be perfect—just as your Father in heaven is perfect.

5.27 Ex 20.14; Dt 5.18 **5.29** Mt 18.9; Mk 9.47 **5.30** Mt 18.8; Mk 9.43 **5.31** Dt 24.1-4; Mt 19.7; Mk 10.4 **5.32** Mt 19.9; Mk 10.11, 12; Lk 16.18; 1 Co 7.10, 11 **5.33 a** Lv 19.12; **b** Nu 30.2; Dt 23.21 **5.34 a** Jas 5.12; **b** Is 66.1; Mt 23.22 **5.35 a** Is 66.1; **b** Ps 48.2 **5.38** Ex 21.24; Lv 24.20; Dt 19.21 **5.48** Lv 19.2; Dt 18.13

Teaching about Charity

6 "Make certain you do not perform your religious duties in public so that people will see what you do. If you do these things publicly, you will not have any reward from your Father in heaven.

2 "So when you give something to a needy person, do not make a big show of it, as the hypocrites do in the houses of worship and on the streets. They do it so that people will praise them. I assure you, they have already been paid

Do not make a big show of it. (6.2)

in full. 3 But when you help a needy person, do it in such a way that even your closest friend will not know about it. 4 Then it will be a private matter. And your Father, who sees what you do in private, will reward you.

Teaching about Prayer
(Luke 11.2-4)

5 "When you pray, do not be like the hypocrites! They love to stand up and pray in the houses of worship and on the street corners, so that everyone will see them. I assure you, they have al-

ready been paid in full. 6 But when you pray, go to your room, close the door, and pray to your Father, who is unseen. And your Father, who sees what you do in private, will reward you.

7 "When you pray, do not use a lot of meaningless words, as the pagans do, who think that their gods will hear them because their prayers are long. 8 Do not be like them. Your Father already knows what you need before you ask him. 9 This, then, is how you should pray:

'Our Father in heaven:
    May your holy name be
        honored;
10   may your Kingdom come;
    may your will be done on
        earth as it is in
        heaven.
11   Give us today the food we
        need. *c*
12   Forgive us the wrongs we
        have done,
        as we forgive the wrongs
        that others have done
        to us.
13   Do not bring us to hard
        testing,
        but keep us safe from the
        Evil One.' *d*

14 "If you forgive others the wrongs they have done to you, your Father in heaven will also forgive you. 15 But if you do not forgive others, then your Father will not forgive the wrongs you have done.

Teaching about Fasting

16 "And when you fast, do not put on a sad face as the hypocrites do. They neglect their appearance so that everyone will see that they are fasting. I assure you, they have already been paid in full. 17 When you go without food,

c we need; *or* for today, *or* for tomorrow.   *d* *Some manuscripts add* For yours is the kingdom, and the power, and the glory forever. Amen.
6.1 Mt 23.5   **6.5** Lk 18.10-14   **6.14, 15** Mk 11.25, 26

wash your face and comb your hair, [18]so that others cannot know that you are fasting — only your Father, who is unseen, will know. And your Father, who sees what you do in private, will reward you.

Riches in Heaven
(Luke 12.33, 34)

[19]"Do not store up riches for yourselves here on earth, where moths and rust destroy, and robbers break in and steal. [20]Instead, store up riches for yourselves in heaven, where moths and rust cannot destroy, and robbers cannot break in and steal. [21]For your heart will always be where your riches are.

The Light of the Body
(Luke 11.34-36)

[22]"The eyes are like a lamp for the body. If your eyes are sound, your whole body will be full of light; [23]but if your eyes are no good, your body will be in darkness. So if the light in you is darkness, how terribly dark it will be!

God and Possessions
(Luke 16.13; 12.22-31)

[24]"You cannot be a slave of two masters; you will hate one and love the other; you will be loyal to one and despise the other. You cannot serve both God and money.

[25]"This is why I tell you: do not be worried about the food and drink you need in order to stay alive, or about clothes for your body. After all, isn't life worth more than food? And isn't the body worth more than clothes? [26]Look at the birds: they do not plant seeds, gather a harvest and put it in barns; yet your Father in heaven takes care of them! Aren't you worth much more

than birds? [27]Can any of you live a bit longer[e] by worrying about it?

[28]"And why worry about clothes? Look how the wild flowers grow: they do not work or make clothes for themselves. [29]But I tell you that not even King Solomon with all his wealth had clothes as beautiful as one of these flowers. [30]It is God who clothes the wild grass — grass that is here today and gone tomorrow, burned up in the oven. Won't he be all the more sure to clothe you? What little faith you have!

Aren't you worth much more than birds? (6.26)

[31]"So do not start worrying: 'Where will my food come from? or my drink? or my clothes?' [32](These are the things the pagans are always concerned about.) Your Father in heaven knows that you need all these things. [33]Instead, be concerned above everything else with the Kingdom of God and with what he requires of you, and he will provide you with all these other things. [34]So do not worry about tomorrow; it will have enough worries of its own. There is no need to add to the troubles each day brings.

Judging Others
(Luke 6.37, 38, 41, 42)

7 "Do not judge others, so that God will not judge you, [2]for God will judge you in the same way you judge others, and he will apply to you the

---

[e] live a bit longer; *or* grow a bit taller.
6.19 Jas 5.2, 3   **6.29** 1 K 10.4-7; 2 Ch 9.3-6   **7.2** Mk 4.24

same rules you apply to others. ³ Why, then, do you look at the speck in your brother's eye and pay no attention to the log in your own eye? ⁴ How dare you say to your brother, 'Please, let me take that speck out of your eye,' when you have a log in your own eye? ⁵ You hypocrite! First take the log out of your own eye, and then you will be able to see clearly to take the speck out of your brother's eye.

⁶ "Do not give what is holy to dogs — they will only turn and attack you. Do not throw your pearls in front of pigs — they will only trample them underfoot.

Ask, Seek, Knock
(Luke 11.9-13)

⁷ "Ask, and you will receive; seek, and you will find; knock, and the door will be opened to you. ⁸ For everyone who asks will receive, and anyone who seeks will find, and the door will be opened to those who knock. ⁹ Would any of you who are fathers give your son a stone when he asks for bread? ¹⁰ Or would you give him a snake when he asks for a fish? ¹¹ As bad as you are, you know how to give good things to your children. How much more, then, will your Father in heaven give good things to those who ask him!

¹² "Do for others what you want them to do for you: this is the meaning of the Law of Moses and of the teachings of the prophets.

The Narrow Gate
(Luke 13.24)

¹³ "Go in through the narrow gate, because the gate to hell is wide and the road that leads to it is easy, and there are many who travel it. ¹⁴ But the gate to life is narrow and the way that leads to it is hard, and there are few people who find it.

A Tree and Its Fruit
(Luke 6.43, 44)

¹⁵ "Be on your guard against false prophets; they come to you looking like sheep on the outside, but on the inside they are really like wild wolves. ¹⁶ You will know them by what they do. Thorn bushes do not bear grapes, and briers do not bear figs. ¹⁷ A healthy tree bears good fruit, but a poor tree bears bad fruit. ¹⁸ A healthy tree cannot bear bad fruit, and a poor tree cannot bear good fruit. ¹⁹ And any tree that does not bear good fruit is cut down and thrown in the fire. ²⁰ So then, you will know the false prophets by what they do.

I Never Knew You
(Luke 13.25-27)

²¹ "Not everyone who calls me 'Lord, Lord' will enter the Kingdom of heaven, but only those who do what my Father in heaven wants them to do. ²² When the Judgment Day comes, many will say to me, 'Lord, Lord! In your name we spoke God's message, by your name we drove out many demons and performed many miracles!' ²³ Then I will say to them, 'I never knew you. Get away from me, you wicked people!'

The Two House Builders
(Luke 6.47-49)

²⁴ "So then, anyone who hears these words of mine and obeys them is like a wise man who built his house on rock. ²⁵ The rain poured down, the rivers flooded over, and the wind blew hard against that house. But it did not fall, because it was built on rock. ²⁶ But anyone who hears these words of mine and does not obey them is like a foolish man who built his house on sand. ²⁷ The rain poured down, the rivers flooded over, the wind blew hard

7.12 Lk 6.31   **7.19** Mt 3.10; Lk 3.9   **7.20** Mt 12.33   **7.23** Ps 6.8

against that house, and it fell. And what a terrible fall that was!"

The Authority of Jesus

28 When Jesus finished saying these things, the crowd was amazed at the way he taught. **29** He wasn't like the teachers of the Law; instead, he taught with authority.

Jesus Heals a Man
(Mark 1.40-45; Luke 5.12-16)

8 When Jesus came down from the hill, large crowds followed him. **2** Then a man suffering from a dreaded skin disease came to him, knelt down before him, and said, "Sir, if you want to, you can make me clean."*f*

3 Jesus reached out and touched him. "I do want to," he answered. "Be clean!" At once the man was healed of his disease. **4** Then Jesus said to him, "Listen! Don't tell anyone, but go straight to the priest and let him examine you; then in order to prove to everyone that you are cured, offer the sacrifice that Moses ordered."

Jesus Heals a Roman Officer's Servant
(Luke 7.1-10)

5 When Jesus entered Capernaum, a Roman officer met him and begged for help: **6** "Sir, my servant is sick in bed at home, unable to move and suffering terribly."

7 "I will go and make him well," Jesus said.

8 "Oh no, sir," answered the officer. "I do not deserve to have you come into my house. Just give the order, and my servant will get well. **9** I, too, am a man under the authority of superior officers, and I have soldiers under me. I order this one, 'Go!' and he goes; and I order that one, 'Come!' and he comes; and I

order my slave, 'Do this!' and he does it."

10 When Jesus heard this, he was surprised and said to the people following him, "I tell you, I have never found anyone in Israel with faith like this. **11** I assure you that many will come from the east and the west and sit down with Abraham, Isaac, and Jacob at the feast in the Kingdom of heaven. **12** But those who should be in the Kingdom will be thrown out into the darkness, where they will cry and gnash their teeth." **13** Then Jesus said to the officer, "Go home, and what you believe will be done for you."

And the officer's servant was healed that very moment.

Jesus Heals Many People
(Mark 1.29-34; Luke 4.38-41)

14 Jesus went to Peter's home, and there he saw Peter's mother-in-law sick in bed with a fever. **15** He touched her hand; the fever left her, and she got up and began to wait on him.

16 When evening came, people brought to Jesus many who had demons in them. Jesus drove out the evil spirits with a word and healed all who were sick. **17** He did this to make come true what the prophet Isaiah had said, "He himself took our sickness and carried away our diseases."

The Would-Be Followers of Jesus
(Luke 9.57-62)

18 When Jesus noticed the crowd around him, he ordered his disciples to go to the other side of the lake. **19** A teacher of the Law came to him. "Teacher," he said, "I am ready to go with you wherever you go."

20 Jesus answered him, "Foxes have holes, and birds have nests, but the Son

f MAKE ME CLEAN: *This disease was considered to make a person ritually unclean.*
7.28, 29 Mk 1.22; Lk 4.32   **8.4** Lv 14.1-32   **8.11** Lk 13.29   **8.12** Mt 22.13; 25.30; Lk 13.28   **8.17** Is 53.4

of Man has no place to lie down and rest."
²¹ Another man, who was a disciple, said, "Sir, first let me go back and bury my father."
²² "Follow me," Jesus answered, "and let the dead bury their own dead."

Jesus Calms a Storm
(Mark 4.35-41; Luke 8.22-25)

²³ Jesus got into a boat, and his disciples went with him. ²⁴ Suddenly a fierce storm hit the lake, and the boat was in danger of sinking. But Jesus was asleep. ²⁵ The disciples went to him and woke him up. "Save us, Lord!" they said. "We are about to die!"
²⁶ "Why are you so frightened?" Jesus answered. "What little faith you have!" Then he got up and ordered the winds and the waves to stop, and there was a great calm.
²⁷ Everyone was amazed. "What kind of man is this?" they said. "Even the winds and the waves obey him!"

Jesus Heals Two Men with Demons
(Mark 5.1-20; Luke 8.26-39)

²⁸ When Jesus came to the territory of Gadara on the other side of the lake, he was met by two men who came out of the burial caves there. These men had demons in them and were so fierce that no one dared travel on that road. ²⁹ At once they screamed, "What do you want with us, you Son of God? Have you come to punish us before the right time?"
³⁰ Not far away there was a large herd of pigs feeding. ³¹ So the demons begged Jesus, "If you are going to drive us out, send us into that herd of pigs."
³² "Go," Jesus told them; so they left and went off into the pigs. The whole herd rushed down the side of the cliff into the lake and was drowned.

³³ The men who had been taking care of the pigs ran away and went into the town, where they told the whole story and what had happened to the men with the demons. ³⁴ So everyone from the town went out to meet Jesus; and when they saw him, they begged him to leave their territory.

Jesus Heals a Paralyzed Man
(Mark 2.1-12; Luke 5.17-26)

9 Jesus got into the boat and went back across the lake to his own town, *ᵍ* ² where some people brought to him a paralyzed man, lying on a bed. When Jesus saw how much faith they had, he said to the paralyzed man, "Courage, my son! Your sins are forgiven."
³ Then some teachers of the Law said to themselves, "This man is speaking blasphemy!"
⁴ Jesus perceived what they were thinking, and so he said, "Why are you thinking such evil things? ⁵ Is it easier to say, 'Your sins are forgiven,' or to say, 'Get up and walk'? ⁶ I will prove to you, then, that the Son of Man has authority on earth to forgive sins." So he said to the paralyzed man, "Get up, pick up your bed, and go home!"
⁷ The man got up and went home. ⁸ When the people saw it, they were afraid, and praised God for giving such authority to people.

Jesus Calls Matthew
(Mark 2.13-17; Luke 5.27-32)

⁹ Jesus left that place, and as he walked along, he saw a tax collector, named Matthew, sitting in his office. He said to him, "Follow me."
Matthew got up and followed him.
¹⁰ While Jesus was having a meal in Matthew's house, *ʰ* many tax collectors and other outcasts came and joined

---

ᵍ HIS OWN TOWN: *Capernaum (see 4.13).* Jesus') house.
9.10, 11 Lk 15.1, 2

ʰ in Matthew's house; *or* in his *(that is,*

Jesus and his disciples at the table. ¹¹Some Pharisees saw this and asked his disciples, "Why does your teacher eat with such people?"

¹²Jesus heard them and answered, "People who are well do not need a doctor, but only those who are sick. ¹³Go and find out what is meant by the scripture that says: 'It is kindness that I want, not animal sacrifices.' I have not come to call respectable people, but outcasts."

The Question about Fasting
(Mark 2.18-22; Luke 5.33-39)

¹⁴Then the followers of John the Baptist came to Jesus, asking, "Why is it that we and the Pharisees fast often, but your disciples don't fast at all?"

¹⁵Jesus answered, "Do you expect the guests at a wedding party to be sad as long as the bridegroom is with them? Of course not! But the day will come when the bridegroom will be taken away from them, and then they will fast.

¹⁶"No one patches up an old coat with a piece of new cloth, for the new patch will shrink and make an even bigger hole in the coat. ¹⁷Nor does anyone pour new wine into used wineskins, for the skins will burst, the wine will pour out, and the skins will be ruined. Instead, new wine is poured into fresh wineskins, and both will keep in good condition."

The Official's Daughter and the Woman Who Touched Jesus' Cloak
(Mark 5.21-43; Luke 8.40-56)

¹⁸While Jesus was saying this, a Jewish official came to him, knelt down before him, and said, "My daughter has just died; but come and place your hands on her, and she will live." ¹⁹So Jesus got up and followed him, and his disciples went along with him.

²⁰A woman who had suffered from severe bleeding for twelve years came up behind Jesus and touched the edge of his cloak. ²¹She said to herself, "If only I touch his cloak, I will get well."

"If only I touch his cloak . . ." (9.21)

²²Jesus turned around and saw her, and said, "Courage, my daughter! Your faith has made you well." At that very moment the woman became well.

²³Then Jesus went into the official's house. When he saw the musicians for the funeral and the people all stirred up, ²⁴he said, "Get out, everybody! The little girl is not dead — she is only sleeping!" Then they all started making fun of him. ²⁵But as soon as the people had been put out, Jesus went into the girl's room and took hold of her hand, and she got up. ²⁶The news about this spread all over that part of the country.

Jesus Heals Two Blind Men

²⁷Jesus left that place, and as he walked along, two blind men started following him. "Have mercy on us, Son of David!" they shouted.

²⁸When Jesus had gone indoors, the two blind men came to him, and he asked them, "Do you believe that I can heal you?"

"Yes, sir!" they answered.

²⁹Then Jesus touched their eyes and

9.13 a Mt 12.7; **b** Ho 6.6

said, "Let it happen, then, just as you believe!" — 30 and their sight was restored. Jesus spoke sternly to them, "Don't tell this to anyone!"

31 But they left and spread the news about Jesus all over that part of the country.

Jesus Heals a Man Who Could Not Speak

32 As the men were leaving, some people brought to Jesus a man who could not talk because he had a demon. 33 But as soon as the demon was driven out, the man started talking, and everyone was amazed. "We have never seen anything like this in Israel!" they exclaimed.

34 But the Pharisees said, "It is the chief of the demons who gives Jesus the power to drive out demons."

Jesus Has Pity for the People

35 Jesus went around visiting all the towns and villages. He taught in the synagogues, preached the Good News about the Kingdom, and healed people with every kind of disease and sickness. 36 As he saw the crowds, his heart was filled with pity for them, because they were worried and helpless, like sheep without a shepherd. 37 So he said to his disciples, "The harvest is large, but there are few workers to gather it in. 38 Pray to the owner of the harvest that he will send out workers to gather in his harvest."

The Twelve Apostles
(Mark 3.13-19; Luke 6.12-16)

10 Jesus called his twelve disciples together and gave them authority to drive out evil spirits and to heal every disease and every sickness.

2 These are the names of the twelve apostles: first, Simon (called Peter) and his brother Andrew; James and his brother John, the sons of Zebedee; 3 Philip and Bartholomew; Thomas and Matthew, the tax collector; James son of Alphaeus, and Thaddaeus; 4 Simon the Patriot, and Judas Iscariot, who betrayed Jesus.

The Mission of the Twelve
(Mark 6.7-13; Luke 9.1-6)

5 These twelve men were sent out by Jesus with the following instructions: "Do not go to any Gentile territory or any Samaritan towns. 6 Instead, you are to go to the lost sheep of the people of Israel. 7 Go and preach, 'The Kingdom of heaven is near!' 8 Heal the sick, bring the dead back to life, heal those who suffer from dreaded skin diseases, and drive out demons. You have received without paying, so give without being paid. 9 Do not carry any gold, silver, or copper money in your pockets; 10 do not carry a beggar's bag for the trip or an extra shirt or shoes or a walking stick. Workers should be given what they need.

11 "When you come to a town or village, go in and look for someone who is willing to welcome you, and stay with him until you leave that place. 12 When you go into a house, say, 'Peace be with you.' 13 If the people in that house welcome you, let your greeting of peace remain; but if they do not welcome you, then take back your greeting. 14 And if some home or town will not welcome you or listen to you, then leave that place and shake the dust off your feet. 15 I assure you that on the Judgment Day God will show more mercy to the people of Sodom and Gomorrah than to the people of that town!

9.34 Mt 10.25; 12.24; Mk 3.22; Lk 11.15   **9.35** Mt 4.23; Mk 1.39; Lk 4.44
9.36 Nu 27.17; 1 K 22.17; 2 Ch 18.16; Ez 34.5; Mk 6.34   **9.37, 38** Lk 10.2
10.10 1 Co 9.14; 1 Ti 5.18   **10.14** Ac 13.51   **10.15 a** Mt 11.24; **b** Gn 19.24-28
10.7-15 Lk 10.4-12

Coming Persecutions
(Mark 13.9-13; Luke 21.12-17)

16 "Listen! I am sending you out just like sheep to a pack of wolves. You must be as cautious as snakes and as gentle as doves. 17 Watch out, for there will be those who will arrest you and take you to court, and they will whip you in the synagogues. 18 For my sake you will be brought to trial before rulers and kings, to tell the Good News to them and to the Gentiles. 19 When they bring you to trial, do not worry about what you are going to say or how you will say it; when the time comes, you will be given what you will say. 20 For the words you will speak will not be yours; they will come from the Spirit of your Father speaking through you.

21 "People will hand over their own brothers to be put to death, and fathers will do the same to their children; children will turn against their parents and have them put to death. 22 Everyone will hate you because of me. But whoever holds out to the end will be saved. 23 When they persecute you in one town, run away to another one. I assure you that you will not finish your work in all the towns of Israel before the Son of Man comes.

24 "No pupil is greater than his teacher; no slave is greater than his master. 25 So a pupil should be satisfied to become like his teacher, and a slave like his master. If the head of the family is called Beelzebul, the members of the family will be called even worse names!

Whom to Fear
(Luke 12.2-7)

26 "So do not be afraid of people. Whatever is now covered up will be uncovered, and every secret will be made known. 27 What I am telling you in the dark you must repeat in broad daylight, and what you have heard in private you must announce from the housetops. 28 Do not be afraid of those who kill the body but cannot kill the soul; rather be afraid of God, who can destroy both body and soul in hell. 29 For only a penny you can buy two sparrows, yet not one sparrow falls to the ground without your Father's consent. 30 As for you, even the hairs of your head have all been counted. 31 So do not be afraid; you are worth much more than many sparrows!

Confessing and Rejecting Christ
(Luke 12.8, 9)

32 "Those who declare publicly that they belong to me, I will do the same for them before my Father in heaven. 33 But those who reject me publicly, I will reject before my Father in heaven.

Not Peace, but a Sword
(Luke 12.51-53; 14.26, 27)

34 "Do not think that I have come to bring peace to the world. No, I did not come to bring peace, but a sword. 35 I came to set sons against their fathers, daughters against their mothers, daughters-in-law against their mothers-in-law; 36 your worst enemies will be the members of your own family.

37 "Those who love their father or mother more than me are not fit to be my disciples; those who love their son or daughter more than me are not fit to be my disciples. 38 Those who do not take up their cross and follow in my steps are not fit to be my disciples. 39 Those who try to gain their own life

---

10.16 Lk 10.3　**10.17-20** Mk 13.9-11; Lk 12.11, 12; 21.12-15　**10.21** Mk 13.12; Lk 21.16
10.22 a Mt 24.9; Mk 13.13; Lk 21.17; **b** Mt 24.13; Mk 13.13　**10.24 a** Lk 6.40; **b** Jn 13.16;
15.20　**10.25** Mt 9.34; 12.24; Mk 3.22; Lk 11.15　**10.26** Mk 4.22; Lk 8.17
10.33 2 Ti 2.12　**10.35, 36** Mic 7.6　**10.38** Mt 16.24; Mk 8.34; Lk 9.23　**10.39** Mt 16.25;
Mk 8.35; Lk 9.24; 17.33; Jn 12.25

will lose it; but those who lose their life for my sake will gain it.

Rewards
(Mark 9.41)

40"Whoever welcomes you welcomes me; and whoever welcomes me welcomes the one who sent me. **41**Whoever welcomes God's messenger because he is God's messenger, will share in his reward. And whoever welcomes a good man because he is good, will share in his reward. **42**You can be sure that whoever gives even a drink of cold water to one of the least of these my followers because he is my follower, will certainly receive a reward."

The Messengers from John the Baptist
(Luke 7.18-35)

11 When Jesus finished giving these instructions to his twelve disciples, he left that place and went off to teach and preach in the towns near there.

2When John the Baptist heard in prison about the things that Christ was doing, he sent some of his disciples to him. **3**"Tell us," they asked Jesus, "are you the one John said was going to come, or should we expect someone else?"

4Jesus answered, "Go back and tell John what you are hearing and seeing: **5**the blind can see, the lame can walk, those who suffer from dreaded skin diseases are made clean,[i] the deaf hear, the dead are brought back to life, and the Good News is preached to the poor. **6**How happy are those who have no doubts about me!"

7While John's disciples were leaving, Jesus spoke about him to the crowds: "When you went out to John in the desert, what did you expect to see? A blade of grass bending in the wind? **8**What did you go out to see? A man dressed up in fancy clothes? People who dress like that live in palaces! **9**Tell me, what did you go out to see? A prophet? Yes indeed, but you saw much more than a prophet. **10**For John is the one of whom the scripture says: 'God said, I will send my messenger ahead of you to open the way for you.' **11**I assure you that John the Baptist is greater than anyone who has ever lived. But the one who is least in the Kingdom of heaven is greater than John. **12**From the time John preached his message until this very day the Kingdom of heaven has suffered violent attacks,[j] and violent men try to seize it. **13**Until the time of John all the prophets and the Law of Moses spoke about the Kingdom; **14**and if you are willing to believe their message, John is Elijah, whose coming was predicted. **15**Listen, then, if you have ears!

16"Now, to what can I compare the people of this day? They are like children sitting in the marketplace. One group shouts to the other, **17**'We played wedding music for you, but you wouldn't dance! We sang funeral songs, but you wouldn't cry!' **18**When John came, he fasted and drank no wine, and everyone said, 'He has a demon in him!' **19**When the Son of Man came, he ate and drank, and everyone said, 'Look at this man! He is a glutton and wine drinker, a friend of tax collectors and other outcasts!' God's wisdom, however, is shown to be true by its results."

The Unbelieving Towns
(Luke 10.13-15)

20The people in the towns where Jesus had performed most of his mira-

---

i MADE CLEAN: *See 8.2.*   *j* has suffered violent attacks; *or* has been coming violently.
10.40 a Lk 10.16; Jn 13.20; **b** Mk 9.37; Lk 9.48   **11.5 a** Is 35.5, 6; **b** Is 61.1   **11.10** Ml 3.1
11.12, 13 Lk 16.16   **11.14** Ml 4.5; Mt 17.10-13; Mk 9.11-13

cles did not turn from their sins, so he reproached those towns. 21"How terrible it will be for you, Chorazin! How terrible for you too, Bethsaida! If the miracles which were performed in you had been performed in Tyre and Sidon, the people there would have long ago put on sackcloth and sprinkled ashes on themselves, to show that they had turned from their sins! 22I assure you that on the Judgment Day God will show more mercy to the people of Tyre and Sidon than to you! 23And as for you, Capernaum! Did you want to lift yourself up to heaven? You will be thrown down to hell! If the miracles which were performed in you had been performed in Sodom, it would still be in existence today! 24You can be sure that on the Judgment Day God will show more mercy to Sodom than to you!"

Come to Me and Rest
(Luke 10.21, 22)

25At that time Jesus said, "Father, Lord of heaven and earth! I thank you because you have shown to the unlearned what you have hidden from the wise and learned. 26Yes, Father, this was how you were pleased to have it happen.

27"My Father has given me all things. No one knows the Son except the Father, and no one knows the Father except the Son and those to whom the Son chooses to reveal him.

28"Come to me, all of you who are tired from carrying heavy loads, and I will give you rest. 29Take my yoke and put it on you, and learn from me, because I am gentle and humble in spirit; and you will find rest. 30For the yoke I will give you is easy, and the load I will put on you is light."

Come to me, all of you who are tired. (11.28)

The Question about the Sabbath
(Mark 2.23-28; Luke 6.1-5)

12 Not long afterward Jesus was walking through some wheat fields on a Sabbath. His disciples were hungry, so they began to pick heads of wheat and eat the grain. 2When the Pharisees saw this, they said to Jesus, "Look, it is against our Law for your disciples to do this on the Sabbath!"

3Jesus answered, "Have you never read what David did that time when he and his men were hungry? 4He went into the house of God, and he and his men ate the bread offered to God, even though it was against the Law for them to eat it — only the priests were allowed to eat that bread. 5Or have you not read in the Law of Moses that every Sabbath the priests in the Temple actually break the Sabbath law, yet they are not guilty? 6I tell you that there is something here greater than the Temple. 7The scripture says, 'It is kindness that I want, not animal sacrifices.' If you really knew what this means, you would not condemn people who are not guilty; 8for the Son of Man is Lord of the Sabbath."

The Man with a Paralyzed Hand
(Mark 3.1-6; Luke 6.6-11)

9Jesus left that place and went to a synagogue, 10where there was a man

---

11.21 Is 23.1-18; Ez 26.1—28.26; Jl 3.4-8; Am 1.9, 10; Zec 9.2-4   **11.23 a** Is 14.13-15;
b Gn 19.24-28   **11.24** Mt 10.15; Lk 10.12   **11.27 a** Jn 3.35; **b** Jn 1.18; 10.15
11.29 Jr 6.16   **12.1** Dt 23.25   **12.3, 4** 1 S 21.1-6   **12.4** Lv 24.9   **12.5** Nu 28.9, 10
12.7 a Mt 9.13; **b** Ho 6.6

who had a paralyzed hand. Some people were there who wanted to accuse Jesus of doing wrong, so they asked him, "Is it against our Law to heal on the Sabbath?"

11 Jesus answered, "What if one of you has a sheep and it falls into a deep hole on the Sabbath? Will you not take hold of it and lift it out? 12 And a human being is worth much more than a sheep! So then, our Law does allow us to help someone on the Sabbath." 13 Then he said to the man with the paralyzed hand, "Stretch out your hand."

He stretched it out, and it became well again, just like the other one. 14 Then the Pharisees left and made plans to kill Jesus.

God's Chosen Servant

15 When Jesus heard about the plot against him, he went away from that place; and large crowds followed him. He healed all the sick 16 and gave them orders not to tell others about him. 17 He did this so as to make come true what God had said through the prophet Isaiah:

18 "Here is my servant, whom I
have chosen,
the one I love, and with
whom I am pleased.
I will send my Spirit upon him,
and he will announce my
judgment to the nations.
19 He will not argue or shout,
or make loud speeches in
the streets.
20 He will not break off a bent reed,
nor put out a flickering lamp.
He will persist until he causes
justice to triumph,
21   and on him all peoples will
put their hope."

Jesus and Beelzebul
(Mark 3.20-30; Luke 11.14-23)

22 Then some people brought to Jesus a man who was blind and could not talk because he had a demon. Jesus healed the man, so that he was able to talk and see. 23 The crowds were all amazed at what Jesus had done. "Could he be the Son of David?" they asked.

24 When the Pharisees heard this, they replied, "He drives out demons only because their ruler Beelzebul gives him power to do so."

25 Jesus knew what they were thinking, and so he said to them, "Any country that divides itself into groups which fight each other will not last very long. And any town or family that divides itself into groups which fight each other will fall apart. 26 So if one group is fighting another in Satan's kingdom, this means that it is already divided into groups and will soon fall apart! 27 You say that I drive out demons because Beelzebul gives me the power to do so. Well, then, who gives your followers the power to drive them out? What your own followers do proves that you are wrong! 28 No, it is not Beelzebul, but God's Spirit, who gives me the power to drive out demons, which proves that the Kingdom of God has already come upon you.

29 "No one can break into a strong man's house and take away his belongings unless he first ties up the strong man; then he can plunder his house.

30 "Anyone who is not for me is really against me; anyone who does not help me gather is really scattering. 31 For this reason I tell you: people can be forgiven any sin and any evil thing they say; *k* but whoever says evil things against the Holy Spirit will not be forgiven. 32 Anyone who says something

k evil thing they say; *or* evil thing they say against God.
12.11 Lk 14.5   **12.18-21** Is 42.1-4 (LXX)   **12.24** Mt 9.34; 10.25
12.30 Mk 9.40   **12.32** Lk 12.10

against the Son of Man can be forgiven; but whoever says something against the Holy Spirit will not be forgiven — now or ever.

A Tree and Its Fruit
(Luke 6.43-45)

33 "To have good fruit you must have a healthy tree; if you have a poor tree, you will have bad fruit. A tree is known by the kind of fruit it bears. 34 You snakes — how can you say good things when you are evil? For the mouth speaks what the heart is full of. 35 A good person brings good things out of a treasure of good things; a bad person brings bad things out of a treasure of bad things.

36 "You can be sure that on the Judgment Day you will have to give account of every useless word you have ever spoken. 37 Your words will be used to judge you — to declare you either innocent or guilty."

The Demand for a Miracle
(Mark 8.11, 12; Luke 11.29-32)

38 Then some teachers of the Law and some Pharisees spoke up. "Teacher," they said, "we want to see you perform a miracle."

39 "How evil and godless are the people of this day!" Jesus exclaimed. "You ask me for a miracle? No! The only miracle you will be given is the miracle of the prophet Jonah. 40 In the same way that Jonah spent three days and nights in the big fish, so will the Son of Man spend three days and nights in the depths of the earth. 41 On the Judgment Day the people of Nineveh will stand up and accuse you, because they turned

from their sins when they heard Jonah preach; and I tell you that there is something here greater than Jonah! 42 On the Judgment Day the Queen of Sheba will stand up and accuse you, because she traveled all the way from her country to listen to King Solomon's wise teaching; and I assure you that there is something here greater than Solomon!

The Return of the Evil Spirit
(Luke 11.24-26)

43 "When an evil spirit goes out of a person, it travels over dry country looking for a place to rest. If it can't find one, 44 it says to itself, 'I will go back to my house.' So it goes back and finds the house empty, clean, and all fixed up. 45 Then it goes out and brings along seven other spirits even worse than itself, and they come and live there. So when it is all over, that person is in worse shape than at the beginning. This is what will happen to the evil people of this day."

Jesus' Mother and Brothers
(Mark 3.31-35; Luke 8.19-21)

46 Jesus was still talking to the people when his mother and brothers arrived. They stood outside, asking to speak with him. 47 So one of the people there said to him, "Look, your mother and brothers are standing outside, and they want to speak with you."[l]

48 Jesus answered, "Who is my mother? Who are my brothers?" 49 Then he pointed to his disciples and said, "Look! Here are my mother and my brothers! 50 Whoever does what my Father in heaven wants is my brother, my sister, and my mother."

[l] *Some manuscripts do not have verse 47.*
12.33 Mt 7.20; Lk 6.44   **12.34 a** Mt 3.7; 23.33; Lk 3.7; **b** Mt 15.18; Lk 6.45
12.38 Mt 16.1; Mk 8.11; Lk 11.16   **12.39** Mt 16.4; Mk 8.12   **12.40** Jon 1.17
12.41 Jon 3.5   **12.42** 1 K 10.1-10; 2 Ch 9.1-12

The Parable of the Sower
(Mark 4.1-9; Luke 8.4-8)

13 That same day Jesus left the house and went to the lakeside, where he sat down to teach. ²The crowd that gathered around him was so large that he got into a boat and sat in it, while the crowd stood on the shore. ³He used parables to tell them many things.

"Once there was a man who went out to sow grain. ⁴As he scattered the seed in the field, some of it fell along the path, and the birds came and ate it up. ⁵Some of it fell on rocky ground, where there was little soil. The seeds soon sprouted, because the soil wasn't deep. ⁶But when the sun came up, it burned the young plants; and because the roots had not grown deep enough, the plants soon dried up. ⁷Some of the seed fell among thorn bushes, which grew up and choked the plants. ⁸But some seeds fell in good soil, and the plants bore grain: some had one hundred grains, others sixty, and others thirty."

⁹And Jesus concluded, "Listen, then, if you have ears!"

The Purpose of the Parables
(Mark 4.10-12; Luke 8.9, 10)

¹⁰Then the disciples came to Jesus and asked him, "Why do you use parables when you talk to the people?"

¹¹Jesus answered, "The knowledge about the secrets of the Kingdom of heaven has been given to you, but not to them. ¹²For the person who has something will be given more, so that he will have more than enough; but the person who has nothing will have taken away from him even the little he has. ¹³The reason I use parables in talking to them is that they look, but do not see, and they listen, but do not hear or understand. ¹⁴So the prophecy of Isaiah applies to them:

'This people will listen and listen,
   but not understand;
they will look and look, but
   not see,
¹⁵because their minds are dull,
   and they have stopped up
     their ears
   and have closed their eyes.
Otherwise, their eyes would see,
   their ears would hear,
   their minds would
     understand,
and they would turn to me,
   says God,
   and I would heal them.'

¹⁶"As for you, how fortunate you are! Your eyes see and your ears hear. ¹⁷I assure you that many prophets and many of God's people wanted very much to see what you see, but they could not, and to hear what you hear, but they did not.

Jesus Explains the Parable of the Sower
(Mark 4.13-20; Luke 8.11-15)

¹⁸"Listen, then, and learn what the parable of the sower means. ¹⁹Those who hear the message about the Kingdom but do not understand it are like the seeds that fell along the path. The Evil One comes and snatches away what was sown in them. ²⁰The seeds that fell on rocky ground stand for those who receive the message gladly as soon as they hear it. ²¹But it does not sink deep into them, and they don't last long. So when trouble or persecution comes because of the message, they give up at once. ²²The seeds that fell among thorn bushes stand for those who hear the message; but the worries about this life and the love for riches choke the message, and they don't bear fruit. ²³And the seeds sown in the good soil stand for those who hear the message and understand it: they bear fruit,

---

13.2 Lk 5.1-3   **13.12** Mt 25.29; Mk 4.25; Lk 8.18; 19.26   **13.14, 15** Is 6.9, 10 (LXX)
13.16, 17 Lk 10.23, 24

some as much as one hundred, others sixty, and others thirty."

The Parable of the Weeds

24 Jesus told them another parable: "The Kingdom of heaven is like this. A man sowed good seed in his field. 25 One night, when everyone was asleep, an enemy came and sowed weeds among the wheat and went away. 26 When the plants grew and the heads of grain began to form, then the weeds showed up. 27 The man's servants came to him and said, 'Sir, it was good seed you sowed in your field; where did the weeds come from?' 28 'It was some enemy who did this,' he answered. 'Do you want us to go and pull up the weeds?' they asked him. 29 'No,' he answered, 'because as you gather the weeds you might pull up some of the wheat along with them. 30 Let the wheat and the weeds both grow together until harvest. Then I will tell the harvest workers to pull up the weeds first, tie them in bundles and burn them, and then to gather in the wheat and put it in my barn.' "

The Parable of the Mustard Seed
(Mark 4.30-32; Luke 13.18, 19)

31 Jesus told them another parable: "The Kingdom of heaven is like this. A man takes a mustard seed and sows it in his field. 32 It is the smallest of all seeds, but when it grows up, it is the biggest of all plants. It becomes a tree, so that birds come and make their nests in its branches."

The Parable of the Yeast
(Luke 13.20, 21)

33 Jesus told them still another parable: "The Kingdom of heaven is like this. A woman takes some yeast and mixes it with a bushel of flour until the whole batch of dough rises."

Jesus' Use of Parables
(Mark 4.33, 34)

34 Jesus used parables to tell all these things to the crowds; he would not say a thing to them without using a parable. 35 He did this to make come true what the prophet had said,

"I will use parables when I
    speak to them;
I will tell them things
    unknown since the
    creation of the world."

Jesus Explains the Parable of the Weeds

36 When Jesus had left the crowd and gone indoors, his disciples came to him and said, "Tell us what the parable about the weeds in the field means." 37 Jesus answered, "The man who sowed the good seed is the Son of Man; 38 the field is the world; the good seed is the people who belong to the Kingdom; the weeds are the people who belong to the Evil One; 39 and the enemy who sowed the weeds is the Devil. The harvest is the end of the age, and the harvest workers are angels. 40 Just as the weeds are gathered up and burned in the fire, so the same thing will happen at the end of the age: 41 the Son of Man will send out his angels to gather up out of his Kingdom all those who cause people to sin and all others who do evil things, 42 and they will throw them into the fiery furnace, where they will cry and gnash their teeth. 43 Then God's people will shine like the sun in their Father's Kingdom. Listen, then, if you have ears!

The Parable of the Hidden Treasure

44 "The Kingdom of heaven is like this. A man happens to find a treasure hidden in a field. He covers it up again,

13.35 Ps 78.2

and is so happy that he goes and sells everything he has, and then goes back and buys that field.

The Parable of the Pearl

45 "Also, the Kingdom of heaven is like this. A man is looking for fine pearls, 46 and when he finds one that is unusually fine, he goes and sells everything he has, and buys that pearl.

The Parable of the Net

47 "Also, the Kingdom of heaven is like this. Some fishermen throw their net out in the lake and catch all kinds of fish. 48 When the net is full, they pull it to shore and sit down to divide the fish: the good ones go into the buckets, the worthless ones are thrown away. 49 It will be like this at the end of the age: the angels will go out and gather up the evil people from among the good 50 and will throw them into the fiery furnace, where they will cry and gnash their teeth.

New Truths and Old

51 "Do you understand these things?" Jesus asked them.

"Yes," they answered.

52 So he replied, "This means, then, that every teacher of the Law who becomes a disciple in the Kingdom of heaven is like a homeowner who takes new and old things out of his storage room."

Jesus Is Rejected at Nazareth
(Mark 6.1-6; Luke 4.16-30)

53 When Jesus finished telling these parables, he left that place 54 and went back to his hometown. He taught in the synagogue, and those who heard him were amazed. "Where did he get such wisdom?" they asked. "And what about

his miracles? 55 Isn't he the carpenter's son? Isn't Mary his mother, and aren't James, Joseph, Simon, and Judas his brothers? 56 Aren't all his sisters living here? Where did he get all this?" 57 And so they rejected him.

Jesus said to them, "A prophet is respected everywhere except in his hometown and by his own family." 58 Because they did not have faith, he did not perform many miracles there.

The Death of John the Baptist
(Mark 6.14-29; Luke 9.7-9)

14 At that time Herod, the ruler of Galilee, heard about Jesus. 2 "He is really John the Baptist, who has come back to life," he told his officials. "That is why he has this power to perform miracles."

3 For Herod had earlier ordered John's arrest, and he had him tied up and put in prison. He had done this because of Herodias, his brother Philip's wife. 4 For some time John the Baptist had told Herod, "It isn't right for you to be married to Herodias!" 5 Herod wanted to kill him, but he was afraid of the Jewish people, because they considered John to be a prophet.

6 On Herod's birthday the daughter of Herodias danced in front of the whole group. Herod was so pleased 7 that he promised her, "I swear that I will give you anything you ask for!"

8 At her mother's suggestion she asked him, "Give me here and now the head of John the Baptist on a plate!"

9 The king was sad, but because of the promise he had made in front of all his guests he gave orders that her wish be granted. 10 So he had John beheaded in prison. 11 The head was brought in on a plate and given to the girl, who took it to her mother. 12 John's disciples came, carried away his body, and buried it; then they went and told Jesus.

13.57 Jn 4.44   **14.3, 4** Lk 3.19, 20   **14.4** Lv 18.16; 20.21

Jesus Feeds Five Thousand
(Mark 6.30-44; Luke 9.10-17; John 6.1-14)

¹³When Jesus heard the news about John, he left there in a boat and went to a lonely place by himself. The people heard about it, and so they left their towns and followed him by land. ¹⁴Jesus got out of the boat, and when he saw the large crowd, his heart was filled with pity for them, and he healed their sick.

¹⁵That evening his disciples came to him and said, "It is already very late, and this is a lonely place. Send the people away and let them go to the villages to buy food for themselves."

¹⁶"They don't have to leave," answered Jesus. "You yourselves give them something to eat!"

¹⁷"All we have here are five loaves and two fish," they replied.

¹⁸"Then bring them here to me," Jesus said. ¹⁹He ordered the people to sit down on the grass; then he took the five loaves and the two fish, looked up to heaven, and gave thanks to God. He broke the loaves and gave them to the disciples, and the disciples gave them to the people. ²⁰Everyone ate and had enough. Then the disciples took up twelve baskets full of what was left over. ²¹The number of men who ate was about five thousand, not counting the women and children.

Jesus Walks on the Water
(Mark 6.45-52; John 6.15-21)

²²Then Jesus made the disciples get into the boat and go on ahead to the other side of the lake, while he sent the people away. ²³After sending the people away, he went up a hill by himself to pray. When evening came, Jesus was there alone; ²⁴and by this time the boat was far out in the lake, tossed about by the waves, because the wind was blowing against it. ²⁵Between three and six o'clock in the morning Jesus came to the disciples, walking on the water. ²⁶When they saw him walking on the water, they were terrified. "It's a ghost!" they said, and screamed with fear.

²⁷Jesus spoke to them at once. "Courage!" he said. "It is I. Don't be afraid!"

²⁸Then Peter spoke up. "Lord, if it is really you, order me to come out on the water to you."

²⁹"Come!" answered Jesus. So Peter got out of the boat and started walking on the water to Jesus. ³⁰But when he noticed the strong wind, he was afraid and started to sink down in the water. "Save me, Lord!" he cried.

³¹At once Jesus reached out and grabbed hold of him and said, "What little faith you have! Why did you doubt?"

³²They both got into the boat, and the wind died down. ³³Then the disciples in the boat worshiped Jesus. "Truly you are the Son of God!" they exclaimed.

Jesus Heals the Sick in Gennesaret
(Mark 6.53-56)

³⁴They crossed the lake and came to land at Gennesaret, ³⁵where the people recognized Jesus. So they sent for the sick people in all the surrounding country and brought them to Jesus. ³⁶They begged him to let the sick at least touch the edge of his cloak; and all who touched it were made well.

The Teaching of the Ancestors
(Mark 7.1-13)

15 Then some Pharisees and teachers of the Law came from Jerusalem to Jesus and asked him, ²"Why is it that your disciples disobey the teaching handed down by our ancestors? They don't wash their hands in the proper way before they eat!"

³Jesus answered, "And why do you disobey God's command and follow

your own teaching? [4] For God said, 'Respect your father and your mother,' and 'If you curse your father or your mother, you are to be put to death.' [5] But you teach that if people have something they could use to help their father or mother, but say, 'This belongs to God,' [6] they do not need to honor their father. [m] In this way you disregard God's command, in order to follow your own teaching. [7] You hypocrites! How right Isaiah was when he prophesied about you!

[8] 'These people, says God, honor
me with their words,
but their heart is really far
away from me.
[9] It is no use for them to
worship me,
because they teach human
rules as though they
were my laws!' "

The Things That Make a Person Unclean
(Mark 7.14-23)

[10] Then Jesus called the crowd to him and said to them, "Listen and understand! [11] It is not what goes into your mouth that makes you ritually unclean; rather, what comes out of it makes you unclean."

[12] Then the disciples came to him and said, "Do you know that the Pharisees had their feelings hurt by what you said?"

[13] "Every plant which my Father in heaven did not plant will be pulled up," answered Jesus. [14] "Don't worry about them! They are blind leaders of the blind; and when one blind man leads another, both fall into a ditch."

[15] Peter spoke up, "Explain this saying to us."

[16] Jesus said to them, "You are still no more intelligent than the others.

[17] Don't you understand? Anything that goes into your mouth goes into your stomach and then on out of your body. [18] But the things that come out of the mouth come from the heart, and these are the things that make you ritually unclean. [19] For from your heart come the evil ideas which lead you to kill, commit adultery, and do other immoral things; to rob, lie, and slander others. [20] These are the things that make you unclean. But to eat without washing your hands as they say you should — this doesn't make you unclean."

A Woman's Faith
(Mark 7.24-30)

[21] Jesus left that place and went off to the territory near the cities of Tyre and Sidon. [22] A Canaanite woman who lived

They are blind leaders of the blind. (15.14)

in that region came to him. "Son of David!" she cried out. "Have mercy on me, sir! My daughter has a demon and is in a terrible condition."

[23] But Jesus did not say a word to her. His disciples came to him and begged him, "Send her away! She is following us and making all this noise!"

---

[m] their father; *some manuscripts have* their father or mother.
15.4 a Ex 20.12; Dt 5.16; **b** Ex 21.17; Lv 20.9   **15.8, 9** Is 29.13 (LXX)   **15.14** Lk 6.39
15.18 Mt 12.34

24 Then Jesus replied, "I have been sent only to the lost sheep of the people of Israel."

25 At this the woman came and fell at his feet. "Help me, sir!" she said.

26 Jesus answered, "It isn't right to take the children's food and throw it to the dogs."

27 "That's true, sir," she answered, "but even the dogs eat the leftovers that fall from their masters' table."

28 So Jesus answered her, "You are a woman of great faith! What you want will be done for you." And at that very moment her daughter was healed.

Jesus Heals Many People

29 Jesus left there and went along by Lake Galilee. He climbed a hill and sat down. **30** Large crowds came to him, bringing with them the lame, the blind, the crippled, the dumb, and many other sick people, whom they placed at Jesus' feet; and he healed them. **31** The people were amazed as they saw the dumb speaking, the crippled made whole, the lame walking, and the blind seeing; and they praised the God of Israel.

Jesus Feeds Four Thousand
(Mark 8.1-10)

32 Jesus called his disciples to him and said, "I feel sorry for these people, because they have been with me for three days and now have nothing to eat. I don't want to send them away without feeding them, for they might faint on their way home."

33 The disciples asked him, "Where will we find enough food in this desert to feed this crowd?"

34 "How much bread do you have?" Jesus asked.

"Seven loaves," they answered, "and a few small fish."

35 So Jesus ordered the crowd to sit down on the ground. **36** Then he took the seven loaves and the fish, gave thanks to God, broke them, and gave them to the disciples; and the disciples gave them to the people. **37** They all ate and had enough. Then the disciples took up seven baskets full of pieces left over. **38** The number of men who ate was four thousand, not counting the women and children.

39 Then Jesus sent the people away, got into a boat, and went to the territory of Magadan.

The Demand for a Miracle
(Mark 8.11-13; Luke 12.54-56)

16 Some Pharisees and Sadducees who came to Jesus wanted to trap him, so they asked him to perform a miracle for them, to show that God approved of him. **2** But Jesus answered, "When the sun is setting, you say, 'We are going to have fine weather, because the sky is red.' **3** And early in the morning you say, 'It is going to rain, because the sky is red and dark.' You can predict the weather by looking at the sky, but you cannot interpret the signs concerning these times![n] **4** How evil and godless are the people of this day! You ask me for a miracle? No! The only miracle you will be given is the miracle of Jonah."

So he left them and went away.

The Yeast of the Pharisees and Sadducees
(Mark 8.14-21)

5 When the disciples crossed over to the other side of the lake, they forgot to take any bread. **6** Jesus said to them, "Take care; be on your guard against the yeast of the Pharisees and Sadducees."

7 They started discussing among themselves, "He says this because we didn't bring any bread."

8 Jesus knew what they were saying,

[n] *Some manuscripts do not have the words of Jesus in verses 2-3.*
16.1 Mt 12.38; Lk 11.16   **16.4** Mt 12.39; Lk 11.29   **16.6** Lk 12.1

MATTHEW 16, 17 26

so he asked them, "Why are you discussing among yourselves about not having any bread? What little faith you have! [9] Don't you understand yet? Don't you remember when I broke the five loaves for the five thousand men? How many baskets did you fill? [10] And what about the seven loaves for the four thousand men? How many baskets did you fill? [11] How is it that you don't understand that I was not talking to you about bread? Guard yourselves from the yeast of the Pharisees and Sadducees!"

[12] Then the disciples understood that he was not warning them to guard themselves from the yeast used in bread but from the teaching of the Pharisees and Sadducees.

Peter's Declaration about Jesus
(Mark 8.27-30; Luke 9.18-21)

[13] Jesus went to the territory near the town of Caesarea Philippi, where he asked his disciples, "Who do people say the Son of Man is?"

[14] "Some say John the Baptist," they answered. "Others say Elijah, while others say Jeremiah or some other prophet."

[15] "What about you?" he asked them. "Who do you say I am?"

[16] Simon Peter answered, "You are the Messiah, the Son of the living God."

[17] "Good for you, Simon son of John!" answered Jesus. "For this truth did not come to you from any human being, but it was given to you directly by my Father in heaven. [18] And so I tell you, Peter: you are a rock, and on this rock foundation I will build my church, and not even death will ever be able to overcome it. [19] I will give you the keys of the Kingdom of heaven; what you prohibit on earth will be prohibited in heaven,

and what you permit on earth will be permitted in heaven."

[20] Then Jesus ordered his disciples not to tell anyone that he was the Messiah.

Jesus Speaks about His Suffering and Death
(Mark 8.31 — 9.1; Luke 9.22-27)

[21] From that time on Jesus began to say plainly to his disciples, "I must go to Jerusalem and suffer much from the elders, the chief priests, and the teachers of the Law. I will be put to death, but three days later I will be raised to life."

[22] Peter took him aside and began to rebuke him. "God forbid it, Lord!" he said. "That must never happen to you!"

[23] Jesus turned around and said to Peter, "Get away from me, Satan! You are an obstacle in my way, because these thoughts of yours don't come from God, but from human nature."

[24] Then Jesus said to his disciples, "If any of you want to come with me, you must forget yourself, carry your cross, and follow me. [25] For if you want to save your own life, you will lose it; but if you lose your life for my sake, you will find it. [26] Will you gain anything if you win the whole world but lose your life? Of course not! There is nothing you can give to regain your life. [27] For the Son of Man is about to come in the glory of his Father with his angels, and then he will reward each one according to his deeds. [28] I assure you that there are some here who will not die until they have seen the Son of Man come as King."

The Transfiguration
(Mark 9.2-13; Luke 9.28-36)

17 Six days later Jesus took with him Peter and the brothers James and John and led them up

16.9 Mt 14.17-21 **16.10** Mt 15.34-38 **16.14** Mt 14.1, 2; Mk 6.14, 15; Lk 9.7, 8 **16.16** Jn 6.68, 69 **16.19** Mt 18.18; Jn 20.23 **16.24** Mt 10.38; Lk 14.27 **16.25** Mt 10.39; Lk 17.33; Jn 12.25 **16.27 a** Mt 25.31; **b** Ps 62.12; Ro 2.6

a high mountain where they were alone. ²As they looked on, a change came over Jesus: his face was shining like the sun, and his clothes were dazzling white. ³Then the three disciples saw Moses and Elijah talking with Jesus. ⁴So Peter spoke up and said to Jesus, "Lord, how good it is that we are here! If you wish, I will make three tents here, one for you, one for Moses, and one for Elijah."

⁵While he was talking, a shining cloud came over them, and a voice from the cloud said, "This is my own dear Son, with whom I am pleased — listen to him!"

⁶When the disciples heard the voice, they were so terrified that they threw themselves face downward on the ground. ⁷Jesus came to them and touched them. "Get up," he said. "Don't be afraid!" ⁸So they looked up and saw no one there but Jesus.

⁹As they came down the mountain, Jesus ordered them, "Don't tell anyone about this vision you have seen until the Son of Man has been raised from death."

¹⁰Then the disciples asked Jesus, "Why do the teachers of the Law say that Elijah has to come first?"

¹¹"Elijah is indeed coming first," answered Jesus, "and he will get everything ready. ¹²But I tell you that Elijah has already come and people did not recognize him, but treated him just as they pleased. In the same way they will also mistreat the Son of Man."

¹³Then the disciples understood that he was talking to them about John the Baptist.

Jesus Heals a Boy with a Demon
(Mark 9.14-29; Luke 9.37-43a)

¹⁴When they returned to the crowd, a man came to Jesus, knelt before him, ¹⁵and said, "Sir, have mercy on my son! He is an epileptic and has such terrible attacks that he often falls in the fire or into water. ¹⁶I brought him to your disciples, but they could not heal him."

¹⁷Jesus answered, "How unbelieving and wrong you people are! How long must I stay with you? How long do I have to put up with you? Bring the boy here to me!" ¹⁸Jesus gave a command to the demon, and it went out of the boy, and at that very moment he was healed.

¹⁹Then the disciples came to Jesus in private and asked him, "Why couldn't we drive the demon out?"

²⁰"It was because you do not have enough faith," answered Jesus. "I assure you that if you have faith as big as a mustard seed, you can say to this hill, 'Go from here to there!' and it will go. You could do anything!"ᵒ

Jesus Speaks Again about His Death
(Mark 9.30-32; Luke 9.43b-45)

²²When the disciples all came together in Galilee, Jesus said to them, "The Son of Man is about to be handed over to those ²³who will kill him; but three days later he will be raised to life."

The disciples became very sad.

Payment of the Temple Tax

²⁴When Jesus and his disciples came to Capernaum, the collectors of the Temple tax came to Peter and asked, "Does your teacher pay the Temple tax?"

²⁵"Of course," Peter answered.

ᵒ *Some manuscripts add verse 21:* But only prayer and fasting can drive this kind out; nothing else can *(see Mk 9.29).*

17.5 a Gn 22.2; Ps 2.7; Is 42.1; Mt 3.17; 12.18; Mk 1.11; Lk 3.22; **b** Dt 18.15
17.1-5 2 P 1.17, 18   **17.10** Ml 4.5   **17.12** Mt 11.14   **17.20** Mt 21.21; Mk 11.23; 1 Co 13.2
17.24 Ex 30.13; 38.26

When Peter went into the house, Jesus spoke up first, "Simon, what is your opinion? Who pays duties or taxes to the kings of this world? The citizens of the country or the foreigners?"

²⁶"The foreigners," answered Peter.

"Well, then," replied Jesus, "that means that the citizens don't have to pay. ²⁷But we don't want to offend these people. So go to the lake and drop in a line. Pull up the first fish you hook, and in its mouth you will find a coin worth enough for my Temple tax and yours. Take it and pay them our taxes."

Who Is the Greatest?
(Mark 9.33-37; Luke 9.46-48)

18 At that time the disciples came to Jesus, asking, "Who is the greatest in the Kingdom of heaven?"

²So Jesus called a child to come and stand in front of them, ³and said, "I assure you that unless you change and

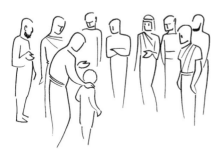

"Unless you change and become like children . . ." (18.3)

become like children, you will never enter the Kingdom of heaven. ⁴The greatest in the Kingdom of heaven is the one who humbles himself and becomes like

this child. ⁵And whoever welcomes in my name one such child as this, welcomes me.

Temptations to Sin
(Mark 9.42-48; Luke 17.1, 2)

⁶"If anyone should cause one of these little ones to lose his faith in me, it would be better for that person to have a large millstone tied around his neck and be drowned in the deep sea. ⁷How terrible for the world that there are things that make people lose their faith! Such things will always happen — but how terrible for the one who causes them!

⁸"If your hand or your foot makes you lose your faith, cut it off and throw it away! It is better for you to enter life without a hand or a foot than to keep both hands and both feet and be thrown into the eternal fire. ⁹And if your eye makes you lose your faith, take it out and throw it away! It is better for you to enter life with only one eye than to keep both eyes and be thrown into the fire of hell.

The Parable of the Lost Sheep
(Luke 15.3-7)

¹⁰"See that you don't despise any of these little ones. Their angels in heaven, I tell you, are always in the presence of my Father in heaven.ᵖ

¹²"What do you think a man does who has one hundred sheep and one of them gets lost? He will leave the other ninety-nine grazing on the hillside and go and look for the lost sheep. ¹³When he finds it, I tell you, he feels far happier over this one sheep than over the ninety-nine that did not get lost. ¹⁴In just the same way yourᵍ Father in heaven does not want any of these little ones to be lost.

ᵖ *Some manuscripts add verse 11:* For the Son of Man came to save the lost (*see Lk 19.10*). ᵍ your; *some manuscripts have* my.
18.1 Lk 22.24   **18.3** Mk 10.15; Lk 18.17   **18.8** Mt 5.30   **18.9** Mt 5.29   **18.11** Lk 19.10

He will . . . go and look for the lost sheep.
(18.12)

When Someone Sins

¹⁵"If your brother sins against you,ʳ go to him and show him his fault. But do it privately, just between yourselves. If he listens to you, you have won your brother back. ¹⁶But if he will not listen to you, take one or two other persons with you, so that 'every accusation may be upheld by the testimony of two or more witnesses,' as the scripture says. ¹⁷And if he will not listen to them, then tell the whole thing to the church. Finally, if he will not listen to the church, treat him as though he were a pagan or a tax collector.

Prohibiting and Permitting

¹⁸"And so I tell all of you: what you prohibit on earth will be prohibited in heaven, and what you permit on earth will be permitted in heaven.

¹⁹"And I tell you more: whenever two of you on earth agree about anything you pray for, it will be done for you by my Father in heaven. ²⁰For where two or three come together in my name, I am there with them."

The Parable of
the Unforgiving Servant

²¹Then Peter came to Jesus and asked, "Lord, if my brother keeps on sinning against me, how many times do I have to forgive him? Seven times?"

²²"No, not seven times," answered Jesus, "but seventy times seven,ˢ ²³because the Kingdom of heaven is like this. Once there was a king who decided to check on his servants' accounts. ²⁴He had just begun to do so when one of them was brought in who owed him millions of dollars. ²⁵The servant did not have enough to pay his debt, so the king ordered him to be sold as a slave, with his wife and his children and all that he had, in order to pay the debt. ²⁶The servant fell on his knees before the king. 'Be patient with me,' he begged, 'and I will pay you everything!' ²⁷The king felt sorry for him, so he forgave him the debt and let him go.

²⁸"Then the man went out and met one of his fellow servants who owed him a few dollars. He grabbed him and started choking him. 'Pay back what you owe me!' he said. ²⁹His fellow servant fell down and begged him, 'Be patient with me, and I will pay you back!' ³⁰But he refused; instead, he had him thrown into jail until he should pay the debt. ³¹When the other servants saw what had happened, they were very upset and went to the king and told him everything. ³²So he called the servant in. 'You worthless slave!' he said. 'I forgave you the whole amount you owed me, just because you asked me to. ³³You should have had mercy on your fellow servant, just as I had mercy on

---

you.' 34 The king was very angry, and he sent the servant to jail to be punished until he should pay back the whole amount."

35 And Jesus concluded, "That is how my Father in heaven will treat every one of you unless you forgive your brother from your heart."

Jesus Teaches about Divorce
(Mark 10.1-12)

19 When Jesus finished saying these things, he left Galilee and went to the territory of Judea on the other side of the Jordan River. 2 Large crowds followed him, and he healed them there.

3 Some Pharisees came to him and tried to trap him by asking, "Does our Law allow a man to divorce his wife for whatever reason he wishes?"

4 Jesus answered, "Haven't you read the scripture that says that in the beginning the Creator made people male and female? 5 And God said, 'For this reason a man will leave his father and mother and unite with his wife, and the two will become one.' 6 So they are no longer two, but one. No human being must separate, then, what God has joined together."

7 The Pharisees asked him, "Why, then, did Moses give the law for a man to hand his wife a divorce notice and send her away?"

8 Jesus answered, "Moses gave you permission to divorce your wives because you are so hard to teach. But it was not like that at the time of creation. 9 I tell you, then, that any man who divorces his wife for any cause other than her unfaithfulness, commits adultery if he marries some other woman."

10 His disciples said to him, "If this is how it is between a man and his wife, it is better not to marry."

11 Jesus answered, "This teaching does not apply to everyone, but only to those to whom God has given it. 12 For there are different reasons why men cannot marry: some, because they were born that way; others, because men made them that way; and others do not marry for the sake of the Kingdom of heaven. Let him who can accept this teaching do so."

Jesus Blesses Little Children
(Mark 10.13-16; Luke 18.15-17)

13 Some people brought children to Jesus for him to place his hands on them and to pray for them, but the disciples scolded the people. 14 Jesus said, "Let the children come to me and do not stop them, because the Kingdom of heaven belongs to such as these."

15 He placed his hands on them and then went away.

The Rich Young Man
(Mark 10.17-31; Luke 18.18-30)

16 Once a man came to Jesus. "Teacher," he asked, "what good thing must I do to receive eternal life?"

17 "Why do you ask me concerning what is good?" answered Jesus. "There is only One who is good. Keep the commandments if you want to enter life."

18 "What commandments?" he asked.

Jesus answered, "Do not commit murder; do not commit adultery; do not steal; do not accuse anyone falsely; 19 respect your father and your mother; and love your neighbor as you love yourself."

20 "I have obeyed all these commandments," the young man replied. "What else do I need to do?"

21 Jesus said to him, "If you want to be perfect, go and sell all you have and give the money to the poor, and you will

19.4 Gn 1.27; 5.2   **19.5** Gn 2.24   **19.7** Dt 24.1-4; Mt 5.31   **19.9** Mt 5.32; 1 Co 7.10, 11
19.18 a Ex 20.13; Dt 5.17; **b** Ex 20.14; Dt 5.18; **c** Ex 20.15; Dt 5.19; **d** Ex 20.16; Dt 5.20
19.19 a Ex 20.12; Dt 5.16; **b** Lv 19.18

have riches in heaven; then come and follow me."

²²When the young man heard this, he went away sad, because he was very rich.

²³Jesus then said to his disciples, "I assure you: it will be very hard for rich people to enter the Kingdom of heaven. ²⁴I repeat: it is much harder for a rich person to enter the Kingdom of God than for a camel to go through the eye of a needle."

²⁵When the disciples heard this, they were completely amazed. "Who, then, can be saved?" they asked.

²⁶Jesus looked straight at them and answered, "This is impossible for human beings, but for God everything is possible."

²⁷Then Peter spoke up. "Look," he said, "we have left everything and followed you. What will we have?"

²⁸Jesus said to them, "You can be sure that when the Son of Man sits on his glorious throne in the New Age, then you twelve followers of mine will also sit on thrones, to rule the twelve tribes of Israel. ²⁹And everyone who has left houses or brothers or sisters or father or mother or children or fields for my sake, will receive a hundred times more and will be given eternal life. ³⁰But many who now are first will be last, and many who now are last will be first.

The Workers in the Vineyard

20 "The Kingdom of heaven is like this. Once there was a man who went out early in the morning to hire some men to work in his vineyard. ²He agreed to pay them the regular wage, a silver coin a day, and sent them to work in his vineyard. ³He went out again to the marketplace at nine o'clock and saw some men standing there doing nothing, ⁴so he told them, 'You also go and work in the vineyard, and I will pay you a fair wage.' ⁵So they went. Then at twelve o'clock and again at three o'clock he did the same thing. ⁶It was nearly five o'clock when he went to the marketplace and saw some other men still standing there. 'Why are you wasting the whole day here doing nothing?' he asked them. ⁷'No one hired us,' they answered. 'Well, then, you go and work in the vineyard,' he told them.

⁸"When evening came, the owner told his foreman, 'Call the workers and pay them their wages, starting with those who were hired last and ending with those who were hired first.' ⁹The men who had begun to work at five o'clock were paid a silver coin each. ¹⁰So when the men who were the first to be hired came to be paid, they thought they would get more; but they too were given a silver coin each. ¹¹They took their money and started grumbling against the employer. ¹²'These men who were hired last worked only one hour,' they said, 'while we put up with a whole day's work in the hot sun—yet you paid them the same as you paid us!' ¹³'Listen, friend,' the owner answered one of them, 'I have not cheated you. After all, you agreed to do a day's work for one silver coin. ¹⁴Now take your pay and go home. I want to give this man who was hired last as much as I gave you. ¹⁵Don't I have the right to do as I wish with my own money? Or are you jealous because I am generous?'"

¹⁶And Jesus concluded, "So those who are last will be first, and those who are first will be last."

Jesus Speaks a Third Time about His Death
(Mark 10.32-34; Luke 18.31-34)

¹⁷As Jesus was going up to Jerusalem, he took the twelve disciples aside

---

19.28 a Mt 25.31; **b** Lk 22.30   **19.30** Mt 20.16; Lk 13.30   **20.8** Lv 19.13; Dt 24.15
20.16 Mt 19.30; Mk 10.31; Lk 13.30

and spoke to them privately, as they walked along. [18]"Listen," he told them, "we are going up to Jerusalem, where the Son of Man will be handed over to the chief priests and the teachers of the Law. They will condemn him to death [19]and then hand him over to the Gentiles, who will make fun of him, whip him, and crucify him; but three days later he will be raised to life."

A Mother's Request
(Mark 10.35-45)

[20]Then the wife of Zebedee came to Jesus with her two sons, bowed before him, and asked him for a favor.

[21]"What do you want?" Jesus asked her.

She answered, "Promise me that these two sons of mine will sit at your right and your left when you are King."

[22]"You don't know what you are asking for," Jesus answered the sons. "Can you drink the cup of suffering that I am about to drink?"

"We can," they answered.

[23]"You will indeed drink from my cup," Jesus told them, "but I do not have the right to choose who will sit at my right and my left. These places belong to those for whom my Father has prepared them."

[24]When the other ten disciples heard about this, they became angry with the two brothers. [25]So Jesus called them all together and said, "You know that the rulers of the heathen have power over them, and the leaders have complete authority. [26]This, however, is not the way it shall be among you. If one of you wants to be great, you must be the servant of the rest; [27]and if one of you wants to be first, you must be the slave of the others — [28]like the Son of Man, who did not come to be served, but to serve and to give his life to redeem many people."

Jesus Heals Two Blind Men
(Mark 10.46-52; Luke 18.35-43)

[29]As Jesus and his disciples were leaving Jericho, a large crowd was following. [30]Two blind men who were sitting by the road heard that Jesus was passing by, so they began to shout, "Son of David! Have mercy on us, sir!"

[31]The crowd scolded them and told them to be quiet. But they shouted even more loudly, "Son of David! Have mercy on us, sir!"

[32]Jesus stopped and called them. "What do you want me to do for you?" he asked them.

[33]"Sir," they answered, "we want you to give us our sight!"

[34]Jesus had pity on them and touched their eyes; at once they were able to see, and they followed him.

The Triumphant Entry into Jerusalem
(Mark 11.1-11; Luke 19.28-40; John 12.12-19)

21 As Jesus and his disciples approached Jerusalem, they came to Bethphage at the Mount of Olives. There Jesus sent two of the disciples on ahead [2]with these instructions: "Go to the village there ahead of you, and at once you will find a donkey tied up with her colt beside her. Untie them and bring them to me. [3]And if anyone says anything, tell him, 'The Master[t] needs them'; and then he will let them go at once."

[4]This happened in order to make come true what the prophet had said:

[5]"Tell the city of Zion,
　Look, your king is coming
　　to you!
　He is humble and rides on a
　　donkey
　and on a colt, the foal of a
　　donkey."

[6]So the disciples went and did what Jesus had told them to do: [7]they

---

[t] The Master; *or* Their owner.
20.25, 26 Lk 22.25, 26　**20.26, 27** Mt 23.11; Mk 9.35; Lk 22.26　**21.5** Zec 9.9

brought the donkey and the colt, threw their cloaks over them, and Jesus got on. [8] A large crowd of people spread their cloaks on the road while others cut branches from the trees and spread them on the road. [9] The crowds walking in front of Jesus and those walking behind began to shout, "Praise to David's Son! God bless him who comes in the name of the Lord! Praise be to God!"

"God bless him who comes in the name of the Lord!" (21.9)

[10] When Jesus entered Jerusalem, the whole city was thrown into an uproar. "Who is he?" the people asked.

[11] "This is the prophet Jesus, from Nazareth in Galilee," the crowds answered.

Jesus Goes to the Temple
(Mark 11.15-19; Luke 19.45-48; John 2.13-22)

[12] Jesus went into the Temple and drove out all those who were buying and selling there. He overturned the tables of the moneychangers and the stools of those who sold pigeons, [13] and said to them, "It is written in the Scriptures that God said, 'My Temple will be called a house of prayer.' But you are making it a hideout for thieves!"

[14] The blind and the crippled came to him in the Temple, and he healed them. [15] The chief priests and the teachers of the Law became angry when they saw the wonderful things he was doing and the children shouting in the Temple, "Praise to David's Son!" [16] So they asked Jesus, "Do you hear what they are saying?"

"Indeed I do," answered Jesus. "Haven't you ever read this scripture? 'You have trained children and babies to offer perfect praise.' "

[17] Jesus left them and went out of the city to Bethany, where he spent the night.

Jesus Curses the Fig Tree
(Mark 11.12-14, 20-24)

[18] On his way back to the city early next morning, Jesus was hungry. [19] He saw a fig tree by the side of the road and went to it, but found nothing on it except leaves. So he said to the tree, "You will never again bear fruit!" At once the fig tree dried up.

[20] The disciples saw this and were astounded. "How did the fig tree dry up so quickly?" they asked.

[21] Jesus answered, "I assure you that if you believe and do not doubt, you will be able to do what I have done to this fig

21.9 Ps 118.25, 26   **21.13** Is 56.7; Jr 7.11   **21.16** Ps 8.2 (LXX)   **21.21** Mt 17.20; 1 Co 13.2

tree. And not only this, but you will even be able to say to this hill, 'Get up and throw yourself in the sea,' and it will. ²²If you believe, you will receive whatever you ask for in prayer."

The Question about Jesus' Authority
(Mark 11.27-33; Luke 20.1-8)

²³Jesus came back to the Temple; and as he taught, the chief priests and the elders came to him and asked, "What right do you have to do these things? Who gave you such right?" ²⁴Jesus answered them, "I will ask you just one question, and if you give me an answer, I will tell you what right I have to do these things. ²⁵Where did John's right to baptize come from: was it from God or from human beings?"

They started to argue among themselves, "What shall we say? If we answer, 'From God,' he will say to us, 'Why, then, did you not believe John?' ²⁶But if we say, 'From human beings,' we are afraid of what the people might do, because they are all convinced that John was a prophet." ²⁷So they answered Jesus, "We don't know."

And he said to them, "Neither will I tell you, then, by what right I do these things.

The Parable of the Two Sons

²⁸"Now, what do you think? There was once a man who had two sons. He went to the older one and said, 'Son, go and work in the vineyard today.' ²⁹'I don't want to,' he answered, but later he changed his mind and went. ³⁰Then the father went to the other son and said the same thing. 'Yes, sir,' he answered, but he did not go. ³¹Which one of the two did what his father wanted?"

"The older one," they answered.

So Jesus said to them, "I tell you: the tax collectors and the prostitutes are going into the Kingdom of God ahead of you. ³²For John the Baptist came to you

showing you the right path to take, and you would not believe him; but the tax collectors and the prostitutes believed him. Even when you saw this, you did not later change your minds and believe him.

The Parable of the Tenants in the Vineyard
(Mark 12.1-12; Luke 20.9-19)

³³"Listen to another parable," Jesus said. "There was once a landowner who planted a vineyard, put a fence around it, dug a hole for the wine press, and built a watchtower. Then he rented the vineyard to tenants and left home on a trip. ³⁴When the time came to gather the grapes, he sent his slaves to the tenants to receive his share of the harvest. ³⁵The tenants grabbed his slaves, beat one, killed another, and stoned another. ³⁶Again the man sent other slaves, more than the first time, and the tenants treated them the same way. ³⁷Last of all he sent his son to them. 'Surely they will respect my son,' he said. ³⁸But when the tenants saw the son, they said to themselves, 'This is the owner's son. Come on, let's kill him, and we will get his property!' ³⁹So they grabbed him, threw him out of the vineyard, and killed him.

⁴⁰"Now, when the owner of the vineyard comes, what will he do to those tenants?" Jesus asked.

⁴¹"He will certainly kill those evil men," they answered, "and rent the vineyard out to other tenants, who will give him his share of the harvest at the right time."

⁴²Jesus said to them, "Haven't you ever read what the Scriptures say?
'The stone which the builders
    rejected as worthless
turned out to be the most
    important of all.
This was done by the Lord;
    what a wonderful sight it is!'

21.32 Lk 3.12; 7.29, 30   **21.33** Is 5.1, 2   **21.42** Ps 118.22, 23

[43]"And so I tell you," added Jesus, "the Kingdom of God will be taken away from you and given to a people who will produce the proper fruits."[u]

[45]The chief priests and the Pharisees heard Jesus' parables and knew that he was talking about them, [46]so they tried to arrest him. But they were afraid of the crowds, who considered Jesus to be a prophet.

The Parable of the Wedding Feast
(Luke 14.15-24)

22 Jesus again used parables in talking to the people. [2]"The Kingdom of heaven is like this. Once there was a king who prepared a wedding feast for his son. [3]He sent his servants to tell the invited guests to come to the feast, but they did not want to come. [4]So he sent other servants with this message for the guests: 'My feast is ready now; my steers and prize calves have been butchered, and everything is ready. Come to the wedding feast!' [5]But the invited guests paid no attention and went about their business: one went to his farm, another to his store, [6]while others grabbed the servants, beat them, and killed them. [7]The king was very angry; so he sent his soldiers, who killed those murderers and burned down their city. [8]Then he called his servants and said to them, 'My wedding feast is ready, but the people I invited did not deserve it. [9]Now go to the main streets and invite to the feast as many people as you find.' [10]So the servants went out into the streets and gathered all the people they could find, good and bad alike; and the wedding hall was filled with people.

[11]"The king went in to look at the guests and saw a man who was not wearing wedding clothes. [12]'Friend, how did you get in here without wedding clothes?' the king asked him. But the man said nothing. [13]Then the king told the servants, 'Tie him up hand and foot, and throw him outside in the dark. There he will cry and gnash his teeth.' "

[14]And Jesus concluded, "Many are invited, but few are chosen."

The Question about Paying Taxes
(Mark 12.13-17; Luke 20.20-26)

[15]The Pharisees went off and made a plan to trap Jesus with questions. [16]Then they sent to him some of their disciples and some members of Herod's party. "Teacher," they said, "we know that you tell the truth. You teach the truth about God's will for people, without worrying about what others think, because you pay no attention to anyone's status. [17]Tell us, then, what do you think? Is it against our Law to pay taxes to the Roman Emperor, or not?"

[18]Jesus, however, was aware of their evil plan, and so he said, "You hypocrites! Why are you trying to trap me? [19]Show me the coin for paying the tax!"

They brought him the coin, [20]and he asked them, "Whose face and name are these?"

[21]"The Emperor's," they answered.

So Jesus said to them, "Well, then, pay to the Emperor what belongs to the Emperor, and pay to God what belongs to God."

[22]When they heard this, they were amazed; and they left him and went away.

The Question about Rising from Death
(Mark 12.18-27; Luke 20.27-40)

[23]That same day some Sadducees came to Jesus and claimed that people will not rise from death. [24]"Teacher," they said, "Moses said that if a man who has no children dies, his brother must marry the widow so that they can have

---

[u] *Some manuscripts add verse 44:* Whoever falls on this stone will be cut to pieces; and if the stone falls on someone, it will crush him to dust *(see Lk 20.18).*

22.13 Mt 8.12; 25.30; Lk 13.28   **22.23** Ac 23.8   **22.24** Dt 25.5

children who will be considered the dead man's children. 25 Now, there were seven brothers who used to live here. The oldest got married and died without having children, so he left his widow to his brother. 26 The same thing happened to the second brother, to the third, and finally to all seven. 27 Last of all, the woman died. 28 Now, on the day when the dead rise to life, whose wife will she be? All of them had married her."

29 Jesus answered them, "How wrong you are! It is because you don't know the Scriptures or God's power. 30 For when the dead rise to life, they will be like the angels in heaven and will not marry. 31 Now, as for the dead rising to life: haven't you ever read what God has told you? He said, 32 'I am the God of Abraham, the God of Isaac, and the God of Jacob.' He is the God of the living, not of the dead."

33 When the crowds heard this, they were amazed at his teaching.

The Great Commandment
(Mark 12.28-34; Luke 10.25-28)

34 When the Pharisees heard that Jesus had silenced the Sadducees, they came together, 35 and one of them, a teacher of the Law, tried to trap him with a question. 36 "Teacher," he asked, "which is the greatest commandment in the Law?"

37 Jesus answered, " 'Love the Lord your God with all your heart, with all your soul, and with all your mind.' 38 This is the greatest and the most important commandment. 39 The second most important commandment is like it: 'Love your neighbor as you love yourself.' 40 The whole Law of Moses and the teachings of the prophets depend on these two commandments."

The Question about the Messiah
(Mark 12.35-37; Luke 20.41-44)

41 When some Pharisees gathered together, Jesus asked them, 42 "What do you think about the Messiah? Whose descendant is he?"

"He is David's descendant," they answered.

43 "Why, then," Jesus asked, "did the Spirit inspire David to call him 'Lord'? David said,

44 'The Lord said to my Lord:
    Sit here at my right side
    until I put your enemies
    under your feet.'

45 If, then, David called him 'Lord,' how can the Messiah be David's descendant?"

46 No one was able to give Jesus any answer, and from that day on no one dared to ask him any more questions.

Jesus Warns against the Teachers of the Law and the Pharisees
(Mark 12.38, 39; Luke 11.43, 46; 20.45, 46)

23 Then Jesus spoke to the crowds and to his disciples. 2 "The teachers of the Law and the Pharisees are the authorized interpreters of Moses' Law. 3 So you must obey and follow everything they tell you to do; do not, however, imitate their actions, because they don't practice what they preach. 4 They tie onto people's backs loads that are heavy and hard to carry, yet they aren't willing even to lift a finger to help them carry those loads. 5 They do everything so that people will see them. Look at the straps with scripture verses on them which they wear on their foreheads and arms, and notice how large they are! Notice also how long are the tassels on their cloaks!v 6 They love the best places at feasts and

v TASSELS ON THEIR CLOAKS: *These tassels were worn as a sign of devotion to God (see Nu 15.37-41).*
22.32 Ex 3.6 **22.37** Dt 6.5 **22.39** Lv 19.18 **22.35-40** Lk 10.25-28 **22.44** Ps 110.1
23.5 a Mt 6.1; **b** Dt 6.8; **c** Nu 15.38

They aren't willing even to lift a finger to help them. (23.4)

the reserved seats in the synagogues; [7] they love to be greeted with respect in the marketplaces and to have people call them 'Teacher.' [8] You must not be called 'Teacher,' because you are all equal and have only one Teacher. [9] And you must not call anyone here on earth 'Father,' because you have only the one Father in heaven. [10] Nor should you be called 'Leader,' because your one and only leader is the Messiah. [11] The greatest one among you must be your servant. [12] Whoever makes himself great will be humbled, and whoever humbles himself will be made great.

Jesus Condemns Their Hypocrisy
(Mark 12.40; Luke 11.39-42, 44, 52; 20.47)

[13] "How terrible for you, teachers of the Law and Pharisees! You hypocrites! You lock the door to the Kingdom of heaven in people's faces, but you yourselves don't go in, nor do you allow in those who are trying to enter![w]

[15] "How terrible for you, teachers of the Law and Pharisees! You hypocrites! You sail the seas and cross whole countries to win one convert; and when you succeed, you make him twice as deserving of going to hell as you yourselves are!

[16] "How terrible for you, blind guides! You teach, 'If someone swears by the Temple, he isn't bound by his vow; but if he swears by the gold in the Temple, he is bound.' [17] Blind fools! Which is more important, the gold or the Temple which makes the gold holy? [18] You also teach, 'If someone swears by the altar, he isn't bound by his vow; but if he swears by the gift on the altar, he is bound.' [19] How blind you are! Which is the more important, the gift or the altar which makes the gift holy? [20] So then, when a person swears by the altar, he is swearing by it and by all the gifts on it; [21] and when he swears by the Temple, he is swearing by it and by God, who lives there; [22] and when someone swears by heaven, he is swearing by God's throne and by him who sits on it.

[23] "How terrible for you, teachers of the Law and Pharisees! You hypocrites! You give to God one tenth even of the seasoning herbs, such as mint, dill, and cumin, but you neglect to obey the really important teachings of the Law, such as justice and mercy and honesty. These you should practice, without neglecting the others. [24] Blind guides! You strain a fly out of your drink, but swallow a camel!

[25] "How terrible for you, teachers of the Law and Pharisees! You hypocrites!

---

[w] *Some manuscripts add verse 14:* How terrible for you, teachers of the Law and Pharisees! You hypocrites! You take advantage of widows and rob them of their homes, and then make a show of saying long prayers! Because of this your punishment will be all the worse! *(see Mk 12.40).*

23.11 Mt 20.26, 27; Mk 9.35; 10.43, 44; Lk 22.26   **23.12** Lk 14.11; 18.14   **23.22** Is 66.1; Mt 5.34   **23.23** Lv 27.30

You clean the outside of your cup and plate, while the inside is full of what you have gotten by violence and selfishness. 26 Blind Pharisee! Clean what is inside the cup first, and then the outside will be clean too!

27 "How terrible for you, teachers of the Law and Pharisees! You hypocrites! You are like whitewashed tombs, which look fine on the outside but are full of bones and decaying corpses on the inside. 28 In the same way, on the outside you appear good to everybody, but inside you are full of hypocrisy and sins.

Jesus Predicts Their Punishment
(Luke 11.47-51)

29 "How terrible for you, teachers of the Law and Pharisees! You hypocrites! You make fine tombs for the prophets and decorate the monuments of those who lived good lives; 30 and you claim that if you had lived during the time of your ancestors, you would not have done what they did and killed the prophets. 31 So you actually admit that you are the descendants of those who murdered the prophets! 32 Go on, then, and finish up what your ancestors started! 33 You snakes and children of snakes! How do you expect to escape from being condemned to hell? 34 And so I tell you that I will send you prophets and wise men and teachers; you will kill some of them, crucify others, and whip others in the synagogues and chase them from town to town. 35 As a result, the punishment for the murder of all innocent people will fall on you, from the murder of innocent Abel to the murder of Zechariah son of Berechiah, whom you murdered between the Temple and the altar. 36 I tell you indeed: the punishment for all these murders will fall on the people of this day!

Jesus' Love for Jerusalem
(Luke 13.34, 35)

37 "Jerusalem, Jerusalem! You kill the prophets and stone the messengers God has sent you! How many times I wanted to put my arms around all your people, just as a hen gathers her chicks under her wings, but you would not let me! 38 And so your Temple will be abandoned and empty. 39 From now on, I tell you, you will never see me again until you say, 'God bless him who comes in the name of the Lord.'"

Jesus Speaks of the Destruction of the Temple
(Mark 13.1, 2; Luke 21.5, 6)

24 Jesus left and was going away from the Temple when his disciples came to him to call his attention to its buildings. 2 "Yes," he said, "you may well look at all these. I tell you this: not a single stone here will be left in its place; every one of them will be thrown down."

Troubles and Persecutions
(Mark 13.3-13; Luke 21.7-19)

3 As Jesus sat on the Mount of Olives, the disciples came to him in private. "Tell us when all this will be," they asked, "and what will happen to show that it is the time for your coming and the end of the age."

4 Jesus answered, "Watch out, and do not let anyone fool you. 5 Many men, claiming to speak for me, will come and say, 'I am the Messiah!' and they will fool many people. 6 You are going to hear the noise of battles close by and the news of battles far away; but do not be troubled. Such things must happen, but they do not mean that the end has come. 7 Countries will fight each other; kingdoms will attack one another. There will be famines and earthquakes

---

23.27 Ac 23.3   **23.33** Mt 3.7; 12.34; Lk 3.7   **23.35 a** Gn 4.8; **b** 2 Ch 24.20, 21
23.38 Jr 22.5   **23.39** Ps 118.26

everywhere. [8] All these things are like the first pains of childbirth.

[9] "Then you will be arrested and handed over to be punished and be put to death. Everyone will hate you because of me. [10] Many will give up their faith at that time; they will betray one another and hate one another. [11] Then many false prophets will appear and fool many people. [12] Such will be the spread of evil that many people's love will grow cold. [13] But whoever holds out to the end will be saved. [14] And this Good News about the Kingdom will be preached through all the world for a witness to all people; and then the end will come.

The Awful Horror
(Mark 13.14-23; Luke 21.20-24)

[15] "You will see 'The Awful Horror' of which the prophet Daniel spoke. It will be standing in the holy place." (Note to the reader: understand what this means!) [16] "Then those who are in Judea must run away to the hills. [17] Someone who is on the roof of a house must not take the time to go down and get any belongings from the house. [18] Someone who is in the field must not go back to get a cloak. [19] How terrible it will be in those days for women who are pregnant and for mothers with little babies! [20] Pray to God that you will not have to run away during the winter or on a Sabbath! [21] For the trouble at that time will be far more terrible than any there has ever been, from the beginning of the world to this very day. Nor will there ever be anything like it again. [22] But God has already reduced the number of days; had he not done so, nobody would survive. For the sake of his chosen people, however, God will reduce the days.

[23] "Then, if anyone says to you, 'Look, here is the Messiah!' or 'There he is!' — do not believe it. [24] For false Messiahs and false prophets will appear; they will perform great miracles and wonders in order to deceive even God's chosen people, if possible. [25] Listen! I have told you this ahead of time.

[26] "Or, if people should tell you, 'Look, he is out in the desert!' — don't go there; or if they say, 'Look, he is hiding here!' — don't believe it. [27] For the Son of Man will come like the lightning which flashes across the whole sky from the east to the west.

[28] "Wherever there is a dead body, the vultures will gather.

The Coming of the Son of Man
(Mark 13.24-27; Luke 21.25-28)

[29] "Soon after the trouble of those days, the sun will grow dark, the moon will no longer shine, the stars will fall from heaven, and the powers in space will be driven from their courses. [30] Then the sign of the Son of Man will appear in the sky; and all the peoples of earth will weep as they see the Son of Man coming on the clouds of heaven with power and great glory. [31] The great trumpet will sound, and he will send out his angels to the four corners of the earth, and they will gather his chosen people from one end of the world to the other.

The Lesson of the Fig Tree
(Mark 13.28-31; Luke 21.29-33)

[32] "Let the fig tree teach you a lesson. When its branches become green and tender and it starts putting out leaves, you know that summer is near. [33] In the same way, when you see all these things, you will know that the time is

24.9 Mt 10.22   **24.13** Mt 10.22   **24.15** Dn 9.27; 11.31; 12.11   **24.17, 18** Lk 17.31
24.21 Dn 12.1; Rev 7.14   **24.26, 27** Lk 17.23, 24   **24.28** Lk 17.37   **24.29 a** Is 13.10;
Jl 2.10, 31; 3.15; Rev 6.12; **b** Is 13.10; Ez 32.7; Jl 2.10; 3.15; **c** Is 34.4; Rev 6.13
24.30 Dn 7.13; Zec 12.10-14; Rev 1.7

near, ready to begin.ˣ ³⁴Remember that all these things will happen before the people now living have all died. ³⁵Heaven and earth will pass away, but my words will never pass away.

No One Knows the Day and Hour
(Mark 13.32-37; Luke 17.26-30, 34-36)

³⁶"No one knows, however, when that day and hour will come—neither the angels in heaven nor the Son;ʸ the Father alone knows. ³⁷The coming of the Son of Man will be like what happened in the time of Noah. ³⁸In the days before the flood people ate and drank, men and women married, up to the very day Noah went into the boat; ³⁹yet they did not realize what was happening until the flood came and swept them all away. That is how it will be when the Son of Man comes. ⁴⁰At that time two men will be working in a field: one will be taken away, the other will be left behind. ⁴¹Two women will be at a mill grinding meal: one will be taken away, the other will be left behind. ⁴²Watch out, then, because you do not know what day your Lord will come. ⁴³If the owner of a house knew the time when the thief would come, you can be sure that he would stay awake and not let the thief break into his house. ⁴⁴So then, you also must always be ready, because the Son of Man will come at an hour when you are not expecting him.

The Faithful or the Unfaithful Servant
(Luke 12.41-48)

⁴⁵"Who, then, is a faithful and wise servant? It is the one that his master has placed in charge of the other servants to give them their food at the proper time. ⁴⁶How happy that servant is if his master finds him doing this when he comes home! ⁴⁷Indeed, I tell you, the master will put that servant in charge of all his property. ⁴⁸But if he is a bad servant, he will tell himself that his master will not come back for a long time, ⁴⁹and he will begin to beat his fellow servants and to eat and drink with drunkards. ⁵⁰Then that servant's master will come back one day when the servant does not expect him and at a time he does not know. ⁵¹The master will cut him in piecesᶻ and make him share the fate of the hypocrites. There he will cry and gnash his teeth.

The Parable of the Ten Young Women

25 "At that time the Kingdom of heaven will be like this. Once there were ten young women who took their oil lamps and went out to meet the bridegroom. ²Five of them were foolish, and the other five were wise. ³The foolish ones took their lamps but did not take any extra oil with them, ⁴while the wise ones took containers full of oil for their lamps. ⁵The bridegroom was late in coming, so they began to nod and fall asleep.

⁶"It was already midnight when the cry rang out, 'Here is the bridegroom! Come and meet him!' ⁷The ten young women woke up and trimmed their lamps. ⁸Then the foolish ones said to the wise ones, 'Let us have some of your oil, because our lamps are going out.' ⁹'No, indeed,' the wise ones answered, 'there is not enough for you and for us. Go to the store and buy some for yourselves.' ¹⁰So the foolish ones went off to buy some oil; and while they were gone, the bridegroom arrived. The five who were ready went in with him to the wedding feast, and the door was closed.

¹¹"Later the others arrived. 'Sir, sir! Let us in!' they cried out. ¹²'Certainly

---

ˣ the time is near, ready to begin; *or* he is near, ready to come.   ʸ *Some manuscripts do not have* nor the Son.   ᶻ cut him in pieces; *or* throw him out.
24.37 Gn 6.5-8   **24.39** Gn 7.6-24   **24.43, 44** Lk 12.39, 40   **25.1** Lk 12.35
25.11, 12 Lk 13.25

not! I don't know you,' the bridegroom answered."

13 And Jesus concluded, "Watch out, then, because you do not know the day or the hour.

The Parable of the Three Servants
(Luke 19.11-27)

14 "At that time the Kingdom of heaven will be like this. Once there was a man who was about to leave home on a trip; he called his servants and put them in charge of his property. **15** He gave to each one according to his ability: to one he gave five thousand gold coins, to another he gave two thousand, and to another he gave one thousand. Then he left on his trip. **16** The servant who had received five thousand coins went at once and invested his money and earned another five thousand. **17** In the same way the servant who had received two thousand coins earned another two thousand. **18** But the servant who had received one thousand coins went off, dug a hole in the ground, and hid his master's money.

19 "After a long time the master of those servants came back and settled accounts with them. **20** The servant who had received five thousand coins came in and handed over the other five thousand. 'You gave me five thousand coins, sir,' he said. 'Look! Here are another five thousand that I have earned.' **21** 'Well done, you good and faithful servant!' said his master. 'You have been faithful in managing small amounts, so I will put you in charge of large amounts. Come on in and share my happiness!' **22** Then the servant who had been given two thousand coins came in and said, 'You gave me two thousand coins, sir. Look! Here are another two thousand that I have earned.' **23** 'Well done, you good and faithful servant!' said his master. 'You have

been faithful in managing small amounts, so I will put you in charge of large amounts. Come on in and share my happiness!' **24** Then the servant who had received one thousand coins came in and said, 'Sir, I know you are a hard man; you reap harvests where you did not plant, and you gather crops where you did not scatter seed. **25** I was afraid, so I went off and hid your money in the ground. Look! Here is what belongs to you.' **26** 'You bad and lazy servant!' his master said. 'You knew, did you, that I reap harvests where I did not plant, and gather crops where I did not scatter seed? **27** Well, then, you should have deposited my money in the bank, and I would have received it all back with interest when I returned. **28** Now, take the money away from him and give it to the one who has ten thousand coins. **29** For to every person who has something, even more will be given, and he will have more than enough; but the person who has nothing, even the little that he has will be taken away from him. **30** As for this useless servant — throw him outside in the darkness; there he will cry and gnash his teeth.'

The Final Judgment

31 "When the Son of Man comes as King and all the angels with him, he will sit on his royal throne, **32** and the people of all the nations will be gathered before him. Then he will divide them into two groups, just as a shepherd separates the sheep from the goats. **33** He will put the righteous people at his right and the others at his left. **34** Then the King will say to the people on his right, 'Come, you that are blessed by my Father! Come and possess the kingdom which has been prepared for you ever since the creation of the world. **35** I was hungry and you fed me, thirsty and you gave me a drink; I was a stranger and you received me in your homes, ³⁶naked and you clothed me; I was sick and you took care of me, in prison and you visited me.' ³⁷The righteous will then answer him, 'When, Lord, did we ever see you hungry and feed you, or thirsty and give you a drink? ³⁸When did we ever see you a stranger and welcome you in our homes, or naked and clothe you? ³⁹When did we ever see you sick or in prison, and visit you?' ⁴⁰The King will reply, 'I tell you, whenever you did this for one of the least important of these followers of mine, you did it for me!'

⁴¹"Then he will say to those on his left, 'Away from me, you that are under God's curse! Away to the eternal fire which has been prepared for the Devil and his angels! ⁴²I was hungry but you would not feed me, thirsty but you would not give me a drink; ⁴³I was a stranger but you would not welcome me in your homes, naked but you would not clothe me; I was sick and in prison but you would not take care of me.' ⁴⁴Then they will answer him, 'When, Lord, did we ever see you hungry or thirsty or a stranger or naked or sick or in prison, and we would not help you?' ⁴⁵The King will reply, 'I tell you, whenever you refused to help one of these least important ones, you refused to help me.' ⁴⁶These, then, will be sent off to eternal punishment, but the righteous will go to eternal life."

The Plot against Jesus
(Mark 14.1, 2; Luke 22.1, 2; John 11.45-53)

26 When Jesus had finished teaching all these things, he said to his disciples, ²"In two days, as you know, it will be the Passover Festi-

val, and the Son of Man will be handed over to be crucified."

³Then the chief priests and the elders met together in the palace of Caiaphas, the High Priest, ⁴and made plans to arrest Jesus secretly and put him to death. ⁵"We must not do it during the festival," they said, "or the people will riot."

Jesus Is Anointed at Bethany
(Mark 14.3-9; John 12.1-8)

⁶Jesus was in Bethany at the house of Simon, a man who had suffered from a dreaded skin disease. ⁷While Jesus was eating, a woman came to him with an alabaster jar filled with an expensive perfume, which she poured on his head. ⁸The disciples saw this and became angry. "Why all this waste?" they asked. ⁹"This perfume could have been sold for a large amount and the money given to the poor!"

¹⁰Jesus knew what they were saying, and so he said to them, "Why are you bothering this woman? It is a fine and beautiful thing that she has done for me. ¹¹You will always have poor people with you, but you will not always have me. ¹²What she did was to pour this perfume on my body to get me ready for burial. ¹³Now, I assure you that wherever this gospel is preached all over the world, what she has done will be told in memory of her."

Judas Agrees to Betray Jesus
(Mark 14.10, 11; Luke 22.3-6)

¹⁴Then one of the twelve disciples — the one named Judas Iscariot — went to the chief priests ¹⁵and asked, "What will you give me if I betray Jesus to you?" They counted out thirty silver coins and gave them to him. ¹⁶From then on Judas was looking for a good chance to hand Jesus over to them.

25.46 Dn 12.2   **26.2** Ex 12.1-27   **26.7** Lk 7.37, 38   **26.11** Dt 15.11   **26.15** Zec 11.12

Thirty silver coins (26.15)

Jesus Eats the Passover Meal
with His Disciples
(Mark 14.12-21; Luke 22.7-13, 21-23;
John 13.21-30)

¹⁷On the first day of the Festival of Unleavened Bread the disciples came to Jesus and asked him, "Where do you want us to get the Passover meal ready for you?"

¹⁸"Go to a certain man in the city," he said to them, "and tell him: 'The Teacher says, My hour has come; my disciples and I will celebrate the Passover at your house.' "

¹⁹The disciples did as Jesus had told them and prepared the Passover meal.

²⁰When it was evening, Jesus and the twelve disciples sat down to eat. ²¹During the meal Jesus said, "I tell you, one of you will betray me."

²²The disciples were very upset and began to ask him, one after the other, "Surely, Lord, you don't mean me?"

²³Jesus answered, "One who dips his bread in the dish with me will betray me. ²⁴The Son of Man will die as the Scriptures say he will, but how terrible for that man who will betray the Son of Man! It would have been better for that man if he had never been born!"

²⁵Judas, the traitor, spoke up. "Surely, Teacher, you don't mean me?" he asked.

Jesus answered, "So you say."

The Lord's Supper
(Mark 14.22-26; Luke 22.14-20;
1 Corinthians 11.23-25)

²⁶While they were eating, Jesus took a piece of bread, gave a prayer of thanks, broke it, and gave it to his disciples. "Take and eat it," he said; "this is my body."

²⁷Then he took a cup, gave thanks to God, and gave it to them. "Drink it, all of you," he said; ²⁸"this is my blood, which seals God's covenant, my blood poured out for many for the forgiveness of sins. ²⁹I tell you, I will never again drink this wine until the day I drink the new wine with you in my Father's Kingdom."

³⁰Then they sang a hymn and went out to the Mount of Olives.

Jesus Predicts Peter's Denial
(Mark 14.27-31; Luke 22.31-34;
John 13.36-38)

³¹Then Jesus said to them, "This very night all of you will run away and leave me, for the scripture says, 'God will kill the shepherd, and the sheep of the flock will be scattered.' ³²But after I am raised to life, I will go to Galilee ahead of you."

³³Peter spoke up and said to Jesus, "I will never leave you, even though all the rest do!"

³⁴Jesus said to Peter, "I tell you that before the rooster crows tonight, you will say three times that you do not know me."

³⁵Peter answered, "I will never say that, even if I have to die with you!"

And all the other disciples said the same thing.

Jesus Prays in Gethsemane
(Mark 14.32-42; Luke 22.39-46)

³⁶Then Jesus went with his disciples to a place called Gethsemane, and he

26.23 Ps 41.9   **26.28 a** Ex 24.8; **b** Jr 31.31-34   **26.31** Zec 13.7   **26.32** Mt 28.16

"Take this cup of suffering from me!" (26.39)

said to them, "Sit here while I go over there and pray." ³⁷ He took with him Peter and the two sons of Zebedee. Grief and anguish came over him, ³⁸ and he said to them, "The sorrow in my heart is so great that it almost crushes me. Stay here and keep watch with me."

³⁹ He went a little farther on, threw himself face downward on the ground, and prayed, "My Father, if it is possible, take this cup of suffering from me! Yet not what I want, but what you want."

⁴⁰ Then he returned to the three disciples and found them asleep; and he said to Peter, "How is it that you three were not able to keep watch with me for even one hour? ⁴¹ Keep watch and pray that you will not fall into temptation. The spirit is willing, but the flesh is weak."

⁴² Once more Jesus went away and prayed, "My Father, if this cup of suffering cannot be taken away unless I drink it, your will be done." ⁴³ He returned once more and found the disciples asleep; they could not keep their eyes open.

⁴⁴ Again Jesus left them, went away, and prayed the third time, saying the same words. ⁴⁵ Then he returned to the disciples and said, "Are you still sleeping and resting? Look! The hour has come for the Son of Man to be handed over to the power of sinners. ⁴⁶ Get up, let us go. Look, here is the man who is betraying me!"

The Arrest of Jesus
(Mark 14.43-50; Luke 22.47-53; John 18.3-12)

⁴⁷ Jesus was still speaking when Judas, one of the twelve disciples, arrived. With him was a large crowd armed with swords and clubs and sent by the chief priests and the elders. ⁴⁸ The traitor had given the crowd a signal: "The man I kiss is the one you want. Arrest him!"

⁴⁹ Judas went straight to Jesus and said, "Peace be with you, Teacher," and kissed him.

⁵⁰ Jesus answered, "Be quick about it, friend!"*ᵃ*

Then they came up, arrested Jesus, and held him tight. ⁵¹ One of those who were with Jesus drew his sword and

They could not keep their eyes open. (26.43)

ᵃ Be quick about it, friend!; *or* Why are you here, friend?

struck at the High Priest's slave, cutting off his ear. [52]"Put your sword back in its place," Jesus said to him. "All who take the sword will die by the sword. [53]Don't you know that I could call on my Father for help, and at once he would send me more than twelve armies of angels? [54]But in that case, how could the Scriptures come true which say that this is what must happen?"

[55]Then Jesus spoke to the crowd, "Did you have to come with swords and clubs to capture me, as though I were an outlaw? Every day I sat down and taught in the Temple, and you did not arrest me. [56]But all this has happened in order to make come true what the prophets wrote in the Scriptures."

Then all the disciples left him and ran away.

Jesus before the Council
(Mark 14.53-65; Luke 22.54, 55, 63-71; John 18.13, 14, 19-24)

[57]Those who had arrested Jesus took him to the house of Caiaphas, the High Priest, where the teachers of the Law and the elders had gathered together. [58]Peter followed from a distance, as far as the courtyard of the High Priest's house. He went into the courtyard and sat down with the guards to see how it would all come out. [59]The chief priests and the whole Council tried to find some false evidence against Jesus to put him to death; [60]but they could not find any, even though many people came forward and told lies about him. Finally two men stepped up [61]and said, "This man said, 'I am able to tear down God's Temple and three days later build it back up.'"

[62]The High Priest stood up and said to Jesus, "Have you no answer to give to this accusation against you?" [63]But Jesus kept quiet. Again the High Priest spoke to him, "In the name of the living God I now put you under oath: tell us

if you are the Messiah, the Son of God."

[64]Jesus answered him, "So you say. But I tell all of you: from this time on you will see the Son of Man sitting at the right side of the Almighty and coming on the clouds of heaven!"

[65]At this the High Priest tore his clothes and said, "Blasphemy! We don't need any more witnesses! You have just heard his blasphemy! [66]What do you think?"

They answered, "He is guilty and must die."

[67]Then they spat in his face and beat him; and those who slapped him [68]said, "Prophesy for us, Messiah! Guess who hit you!"

Peter Denies Jesus
(Mark 14.66-72; Luke 22.56-62; John 18.15-18, 25-27)

[69]Peter was sitting outside in the courtyard when one of the High Priest's servant women came to him and said, "You, too, were with Jesus of Galilee."

[70]But he denied it in front of them all. "I don't know what you are talking about," he answered, [71]and went on out to the entrance of the courtyard. Another servant woman saw him and said to the men there, "He was with Jesus of Nazareth."

[72]Again Peter denied it and answered, "I swear that I don't know that man!"

[73]After a little while the men standing there came to Peter. "Of course you are one of them," they said. "After all, the way you speak gives you away!"

[74]Then Peter said, "I swear that I am telling the truth! May God punish me if I am not! I do not know that man!"

Just then a rooster crowed, [75]and Peter remembered what Jesus had told him: "Before the rooster crows, you will say three times that you do not know me." He went out and wept bitterly.

26.55 Lk 19.47; 21.37   **26.61** Jn 2.19   **26.64** Dn 7.13   **26.65, 66** Lv 24.16   **26.67** Is 50.6

Jesus Is Taken to Pilate
(Mark 15.1; Luke 23.1, 2; John 18.28-32)

27 Early in the morning all the chief priests and the elders made their plans against Jesus to put him to death. ²They put him in chains, led him off, and handed him over to Pilate, the Roman governor.

The Death of Judas
(Acts 1.18, 19)

³When Judas, the traitor, learned that Jesus had been condemned, he repented and took back the thirty silver coins to the chief priests and the elders. ⁴"I have sinned by betraying an innocent man to death!" he said.

"What do we care about that?" they answered. "That is your business!"

⁵Judas threw the coins down in the Temple and left; then he went off and hanged himself.

⁶The chief priests picked up the coins and said, "This is blood money, and it is against our Law to put it in the Temple treasury." ⁷After reaching an agreement about it, they used the money to buy Potter's Field, as a cemetery for foreigners. ⁸That is why that field is called "Field of Blood" to this very day.

⁹Then what the prophet Jeremiah had said came true: "They took the thirty silver coins, the amount the people of Israel had agreed to pay for him, ¹⁰and used the money to buy the potter's field, as the Lord had commanded me."

Pilate Questions Jesus
(Mark 15.2-5; Luke 23.3-5; John 18.33-38)

¹¹Jesus stood before the Roman governor, who questioned him. "Are you the king of the Jews?" he asked.

"So you say," answered Jesus. ¹²But he said nothing in response to the accusations of the chief priests and elders. ¹³So Pilate said to him, "Don't you hear all these things they accuse you of?"

¹⁴But Jesus refused to answer a single word, with the result that the Governor was greatly surprised.

Jesus Is Sentenced to Death
(Mark 15.6-15; Luke 23.13-25; John 18.39 — 19.16)

¹⁵At every Passover Festival the Roman governor was in the habit of setting free any one prisoner the crowd asked for. ¹⁶At that time there was a well-known prisoner named Jesus Barabbas. ¹⁷So when the crowd gathered, Pilate asked them, "Which one do you want me to set free for you? Jesus Barabbas or Jesus called the Messiah?" ¹⁸He knew very well that the Jewish authorities had handed Jesus over to him because they were jealous.

¹⁹While Pilate was sitting in the judgment hall, his wife sent him a message: "Have nothing to do with that innocent man, because in a dream last night I suffered much on account of him."

²⁰The chief priests and the elders persuaded the crowd to ask Pilate to set Barabbas free and have Jesus put to death. ²¹But Pilate asked the crowd, "Which one of these two do you want me to set free for you?"

"Barabbas!" they answered.

²²"What, then, shall I do with Jesus called the Messiah?" Pilate asked them.

"Crucify him!" they all answered.

²³But Pilate asked, "What crime has he committed?"

Then they started shouting at the top of their voices: "Crucify him!"

²⁴When Pilate saw that it was no use to go on, but that a riot might break out, he took some water, washed his hands in front of the crowd, and said, "I am not

27.3-8 Ac 1.18, 19   **27.9, 10** Zec 11.12, 13   **27.24** Dt 21.6-9

responsible for the death of this man! This is your doing!"

²⁵The whole crowd answered, "Let the responsibility for his death fall on us and on our children!"

²⁶Then Pilate set Barabbas free for them; and after he had Jesus whipped, he handed him over to be crucified.

The Soldiers Make Fun of Jesus
(Mark 15.16-20; John 19.2, 3)

²⁷Then Pilate's soldiers took Jesus into the governor's palace, and the whole company gathered around him. ²⁸They stripped off his clothes and put a scarlet robe on him. ²⁹Then they made a crown out of thorny branches and placed it on his head, and put a stick in his right hand; then they knelt before him and made fun of him. "Long live the King of the Jews!" they said. ³⁰They spat on him, and took the stick and hit him over the head. ³¹When they had finished making fun of him, they took the robe off and put his own clothes back on him. Then they led him out to crucify him.

Jesus Is Crucified
(Mark 15.21-32; Luke 23.26-43; John 19.17-27)

³²As they were going out, they met a man from Cyrene named Simon, and the soldiers forced him to carry Jesus' cross. ³³They came to a place called Golgotha, which means, "The Place of the Skull." ³⁴There they offered Jesus wine mixed with a bitter substance; but after tasting it, he would not drink it.

³⁵They crucified him and then divided his clothes among them by throwing dice. ³⁶After that they sat there and watched him. ³⁷Above his head they put the written notice of the accusation against him: "This is Jesus, the King of the Jews." ³⁸Then they crucified two bandits with Jesus, one on his right and the other on his left.

³⁹People passing by shook their heads and hurled insults at Jesus: ⁴⁰"You were going to tear down the Temple and build it back up in three days! Save yourself if you are God's Son! Come on down from the cross!"

⁴¹In the same way the chief priests and the teachers of the Law and the elders made fun of him: ⁴²"He saved others, but he cannot save himself! Isn't he the king of Israel? If he will come down off the cross now, we will believe in him! ⁴³He trusts in God and claims to be God's Son. Well, then, let us see if God wants to save him now!"

⁴⁴Even the bandits who had been crucified with him insulted him in the same way.

The Death of Jesus
(Mark 15.33-41; Luke 23.44-49; John 19.28-30)

⁴⁵At noon the whole country was covered with darkness, which lasted for three hours. ⁴⁶At about three o'clock Jesus cried out with a loud shout, *"Eli, Eli, lema sabachthani?"* which means, "My God, my God, why did you abandon me?"

⁴⁷Some of the people standing there heard him and said, "He is calling for Elijah!" ⁴⁸One of them ran up at once, took a sponge, soaked it in cheap wine, put it on the end of a stick, and tried to make him drink it.

⁴⁹But the others said, "Wait, let us see if Elijah is coming to save him!"

⁵⁰Jesus again gave a loud cry and breathed his last.

⁵¹Then the curtain hanging in the Temple was torn in two from top to

---

27.34 Ps 69.21   **27.35** Ps 22.18   **27.39** Ps 22.7; 109.25   **27.40** Mt 26.61; Jn 2.19
27.43 Ps 22.8   **27.46** Ps 22.1   **27.48** Ps 69.21   **27.51** Ex 26.31-33

bottom. The earth shook, the rocks split apart, 52 the graves broke open, and many of God's people who had died were raised to life. 53 They left the graves, and after Jesus rose from death, they went into the Holy City, where many people saw them.

54 When the army officer and the soldiers with him who were watching Jesus saw the earthquake and everything else that happened, they were terrified and said, "He really was the Son of God!"

55 There were many women there, looking on from a distance, who had followed Jesus from Galilee and helped him. 56 Among them were Mary Magdalene, Mary the mother of James and Joseph, and the wife of Zebedee.

The Burial of Jesus
(Mark 15.42-47; Luke 23.50-56; John 19.38-42)

57 When it was evening, a rich man from Arimathea arrived; his name was Joseph, and he also was a disciple of Jesus. 58 He went into the presence of Pilate and asked for the body of Jesus. Pilate gave orders for the body to be given to Joseph. 59 So Joseph took it, wrapped it in a new linen sheet, 60 and placed it in his own tomb, which he had just recently dug out of solid rock. Then he rolled a large stone across the entrance to the tomb and went away. 61 Mary Magdalene and the other Mary were sitting there, facing the tomb.

The Guard at the Tomb

62 The next day, which was a Sabbath, the chief priests and the Pharisees met with Pilate 63 and said, "Sir, we remember that while that liar was still alive he said, 'I will be raised to life three days later.' 64 Give orders, then,

for his tomb to be carefully guarded until the third day, so that his disciples will not be able to go and steal the body, and then tell the people that he was raised from death. This last lie would be even worse than the first one."

65 "Take a guard," Pilate told them; "go and make the tomb as secure as you can."

66 So they left and made the tomb secure by putting a seal on the stone and leaving the guard on watch.

The Resurrection
(Mark 16.1-10; Luke 24.1-12; John 20.1-10)

28 After the Sabbath, as Sunday morning was dawning, Mary Magdalene and the other Mary went to look at the tomb. 2 Suddenly there was a violent earthquake; an angel of the Lord came down from heaven, rolled the stone away, and sat on it. 3 His appearance was like lightning, and his clothes were white as snow. 4 The guards were so afraid that they trembled and became like dead men.

5 The angel spoke to the women. "You must not be afraid," he said. "I know you are looking for Jesus, who was crucified. 6 He is not here; he has been raised, just as he said. Come here and see the place where he was lying. 7 Go quickly now, and tell his disciples, 'He has been raised from death, and now he is going to Galilee ahead of you; there you will see him!' Remember what I have told you."

8 So they left the tomb in a hurry, afraid and yet filled with joy, and ran to tell his disciples.

9 Suddenly Jesus met them and said, "Peace be with you." They came up to him, took hold of his feet, and worshiped him. 10 "Do not be afraid," Jesus said to them. "Go and tell my brothers

27.55, 56 Lk 8.2, 3   **27.63** Mt 16.21; 17.23; 20.19; Mk 8.31; 9.31; 10.33, 34; Lk 9.22; 18.31-33

to go to Galilee, and there they will see me."

The Report of the Guard

11 While the women went on their way, some of the soldiers guarding the tomb went back to the city and told the chief priests everything that had happened. 12 The chief priests met with the elders and made their plan; they gave a large sum of money to the soldiers 13 and said, "You are to say that his disciples came during the night and stole his body while you were asleep. 14 And if the Governor should hear of this, we will convince him that you are innocent, and you will have nothing to worry about."

15 The guards took the money and did what they were told to do. And so that

is the report spread around by the Jews to this very day.

Jesus Appears to His Disciples
(Mark 16.14-18; Luke 24.36-49; John 20.19-23; Acts 1.6-8)

16 The eleven disciples went to the hill in Galilee where Jesus had told them to go. 17 When they saw him, they worshiped him, even though some of them doubted. 18 Jesus drew near and said to them, "I have been given all authority in heaven and on earth. 19 Go, then, to all peoples everywhere and make them my disciples: baptize them in the name of the Father, the Son, and the Holy Spirit, 20 and teach them to obey everything I have commanded you. And I will be with you always, to the end of the age."

28.16 Mt 26.32; Mk 14.28   **28.19** Ac 1.8

Word List

Maps

WORD LIST

This Word List identifies many objects or cultural features whose meaning may not be known to all readers.

Abyss The place in the depths of the earth where the demons were imprisoned until their final punishment.

Agate A semiprecious stone of various colors, but usually white and brown.

Alabaster A soft stone of usually light creamy color, from which vases and jars were made.

Aloes A sweet-smelling substance, derived from a plant. It was used medicinally and as a perfume.

Amen A Hebrew word which means "it is so" or "may it be so." It can also be translated "certainly," "truly," or "surely." In Revelation 3.14 it is used as a title for Christ.

Amethyst A semiprecious stone, usually purple or violet in color.

Anoint To pour or rub olive oil on someone in order to honor him or to appoint him to some special work. The Israelite kings were anointed as a sign of their taking office, and so the king could be called "the anointed one." In a figurative sense, "The Anointed One" is the title of the one whom God chose and appointed as Savior and Lord.

Apostle Principally one of the group of twelve men whom Jesus chose to be his special followers and helpers. It is also used in the New Testament to refer to Paul and other Christians workers. The word may have the sense of "messenger."

Areopagus A hill in Athens where the city council used to meet. For this reason the council itself was called Areopagus, even after it no longer met on the hill.

Artemis The Greek name of an ancient goddess of fertility, worshiped especially in Asia Minor.

Baal The god of fertility worshiped by the Canaanites; his female counterpart was Asherah. After the Hebrews invaded Canaan, many of them began worshiping these two gods.

Barley A cultivated grain similar to wheat, grown as a food crop.

Beelzebul A New Testament name given to the Devil as the chief of the evil spirits.

Beryl A semiprecious stone usually green or bluish green in color.

Breastplate Part of a soldier's armor, made of leather or metal; it covered the chest and sometimes the back as a protection against arrows and the blows of a sword.

Carnelian A semiprecious stone, usually red in color.

Chalcedony A semiprecious stone, usually milky or gray in color.

Christ Originally a title, the Greek equivalent of the Hebrew word "Messiah." It means "the anointed one." Jesus was called the Christ because he was the one whom God chose and sent as Savior and Lord.

Circumcise To cut off the foreskin of the penis. As a sign of God's covenant with his people Israelite boys were circumcised eight days after they were born (Genesis 17.9-14).

Council The supreme religious court of the Jews, composed of seventy leaders of the Jewish people and presided over by the High Priest.

Covenant An agreement, either between persons or between God and a person or a people.

Covenant Box The wooden chest covered with gold, in which were kept the two stone tablets on which were written the Ten Commandments. It has traditionally been called the Ark of the Covenant.

Cumin A small plant whose seeds are ground up and used for seasoning foods.

Dedication, Festival of The Jewish festival, lasting eights days, which celebrated the restoration and rededication in 165 B.C. of the Temple altar by

WORD LIST

the Jewish patriot Judas Maccabeus. The festival began on the 25th day of the month Kislev (around December 10). The Jewish name for this festival is Hanukkah.

Defile To make ritually unclean or impure. Certain foods and practices were prohibited by the Law of Moses because they were thought to make a person ritually or ceremonially unclean. Such persons could not take part in the public worship until they had performed certain rituals which would remove the defilement.

Demon An evil spirit with the power to harm people; it was regarded as a messenger and servant of the Devil.

Dill A small garden plant whose stems, leaves, and seed are used for seasoning food.

Disciple A person who follows and learns from someone else. In the New Testament the word used of the followers of John the Baptist and especially of the followers of Jesus, particularly the twelve apostles.

Dragon A legendary beast, thought to be like a huge lizard. It is also called a serpent and appears as a figure of the Devil (Revelation 12.3–13.4; 20.2,3).

Elders In the Old Testament this is a name given to certain respected leaders of a tribe, nation, or city. In the New Testament three different groups are called elders: (1) in the Gospels the elders are influential Jewish religious leaders, some of whom were members of the supreme Council; (2) in Acts 11–21 and the Letters the elders are Christian church officers who had general responsibility for the work of the church; (3) in Revelation the twenty-four elders are part of God's court in heaven, perhaps as representatives of God's people.

Epicureans Those who followed the teaching of Epicurus (died 270 B.C.), a Greek philosopher who taught that happiness is the highest good in life.

Epileptic A person who suffers from a nervous disease causing convulsions and fainting.

Eunuch A man who has been made physically incapable of having normal sexual relations. Eunuchs were often important officials in the courts of ancient kings, and the term may have come to be used of such officials in general, regardless of their sexual condition.

Fast To go without food for a while as a religious duty.

Frankincense A valuable incense, made from the sap of a certain tree. This incense was probably imported from Arabia.

Gentile A person who is not a Jew.

Hades The Greek name used in the New Testament to refer to the world of the dead.

Harvest Festival The Israelite festival celebrating the wheat harvest, held in the latter part of May, fifty days after Passover. The Jewish name for this festival is Shavuoth (The Feast of Weeks). It has also been called Pentecost.

Hermes The name of a Greek god who served as messenger of the gods.

Herod's party A political party in New Testament times composed of Jews who favored being ruled by one of the descendants of Herod the Great rather than by the Roman governor.

High Priest The priest who occupied the highest office in the Jewish priestly system and was president of the supreme Council of the Jews. Once a year (on the Day of Atonement) he would enter the Most Holy Place in the Temple and offer sacrifice for himself and for the sins of the people of Israel.

Hyssop A small bushy plant, used in religious ceremonies to sprinkle liquids.

Incense Material which is burned in order to produce a pleasant smell. The Israelites used it in their worship.

Jasper A semiprecious stone of various colors. The jasper mentioned in the Bible was probably green, or else clear.

Law The name that the Jews applied to the first five books of the Old Testament, also called "The Books of Moses." Sometimes, however, the name is applied in a more general way to the entire Old Testament.

Levite (1) A member of the tribe of Levi; (2) a man who assisted the priest in the performance of religious duties.

Living creatures (also referred to as "winged creatures" and traditionally called "cherubim") Symbols of God's majesty and associated with his presence. For a description of such creatures see Exodus 25.18-20; Ezekiel 1.5-13; 10; Revelation 4.6-9.

Manna A food eaten by the Israelites during their travels in the wilderness. It was white and flaky and looked like small seeds (Exodus 16.14-21; Numbers 11.7-9)

Messiah A Hebrew title (meaning "the anointed one") given to the promised Savior, whose coming was foretold by the Hebrew prophets; the corresponding Greek term "The Christ" has the same meaning.

Most Holy Place The innermost room of the Tent of the Lord's presence or the Temple. The Covenant Box was kept there. Only the High Priest could enter the Most Holy Place, and he did so only once a year, on the Day of Atonement.

Mustard A large plant which grows from a very small seed. The seeds were ground into powder and used as spice on food.

Myrrh A sweet-smelling resin that was highly priced. It served as a medicine (Mark 15.23) and was used by the Jews to prepare bodies for burial (John 19.39).

Nard An expensive perfume made from a plant.

Nazarene Someone from the town of Nazareth. The name was used as a title for Jesus and also as a name for early Christians (Acts 24.5).

New Moon Festival A religious observance held by the Israelites on the day of each new moon.

Onyx A semiprecious stone of various colors.

Outcasts In the Gospels this name, which in many translations appears as "sinners," refers to those Jews who had been excluded from synagogue worship because they violated rules about foods that should not be eaten and about associating with people who were not Jews. Such outcasts were despised by many of their fellow Jews, and Jesus was criticized for associating with them (Mark 2.15-17; Luke 7.34; 15.1,2).

Parable A story which teaches spiritual truth; such stories were often used by Jesus.

Paradise A name for heaven (Luke 23.43; 2 Corinthians 12.3).

Paralytic Someone who suffers from a disease that prevents him from moving part or all of his body.

Passover The Israelite festival, on the 14th day of the month Nisan (around April 1), which celebrated the deliverance of the ancient Hebrews from their captivity in Egypt. The Angel of Death killed the first-born in the Egyptian homes but passed over the Hebrew homes (Exodus 12.23-27). The Jewish name for this festival is Pesach.

Pentecost, Day of The Greek name for the Israelite festival of wheat harvest (see Harvest Festival). The name Pentecost (meaning "fiftieth") comes from the fact that the feast was held fifty days after Passover.

Pharisees A Jewish religious party during the time of Jesus. They were strict in obeying the Law of Moses and other religious regulations which had been added to it through the centuries.

Preparation, Day of The sixth day of the week (Friday), on which the Jews made the required preparations to observe the Sabbath (Saturday).

Prophet A person who proclaims a message from God. The term usually refers to certain prophets in the Old Testament, but the New Testament speaks of prophets in the early church. John the Baptist is also called a prophet.

Quartz A semiprecious stone of various colors, but usually clear.

Rabbi A Hebrew word which means "my teacher."

Red Sea Evidently referred originally to (1) a series of lakes and marshes between the head of the Gulf of Suez and the Mediterranean, the region generally regarded as the site of the events described in Exodus 13, and was also used to designate (2) the Gulf of Suez, (3) the Gulf of Aqaba.

Rephan The name of an ancient god that was worshiped as the ruler of the planet Saturn.

Sabbath The seventh day of the Jewish week (from sundown on Friday to sundown on Saturday), a holy day in which no work was permitted.

Sackcloth A coarse cloth made of goats' hair, which was worn as a sign of mourning or distress.

Sadducees A small Jewish religious party in New Testament times, composed largely of priests. They based their beliefs primarily on the first five books of the Old Testament and differed in several matters of belief and practice from the larger party of the Pharisees.

Samaritan A name used to refer to a native of Samaria, the region between Judea and Galilee. Because of differences in politics, race, customs, and religion (including especially the central place of worship), there was much bad feeling between the Jews and the Samaritans.

Sapphire A very valuable stone, usually blue in color.

Scorpion A small creature which has eight legs and a long tail with a poisonous sting. It can inflict a very painful, and sometimes fatal, wound.

Scriptures In the New Testament the word refers to the collected body of Hebrew sacred writings, known to Christians as the Old Testament. Various names are used: the Law (or the Law of Moses) and the prophets (Matthew 5.17; Luke 2.22; 24.44; Acts 13.15; 28.23); the Holy Scriptures (Romans 1.2; 2 Timothy 3.15); the old covenant (2 Corinthians 3.14). The singular "scripture" refers to a single passage of the Old Testament.

Serpent A name given to the dragon, which appears in the New Testament as a figure of the Devil (Revelation 12.3-17; 20.2,3).

Shelters, Festival of A joyous festival celebrated by the Israelites in the fall after the completion of the harvest. In order to make them remember the years when their ancestors wandered through the wilderness, the Israelites constructed enough shelters to live in during the festival. The Jewish name for this festival is Sukkoth. It has been traditionally called the Feast of Tabernacles or the Feast of Booths.

Sickle A tool consisting of a curved metal blade and a wooden handle, used for cutting wheat and other crops.

Stoics Those who followed the teachings of the Greek philosopher Zeno (died 265 B.C.), who taught that happiness is to be found in being free from pleasure and pain.

Sulfur In the Bible this refers to a sulfur compound which burns with great heat and produces an unpleasant smell.

Synagogue A place where Jews met every Sabbath day for their public worship. It probably also served as a center for Jewish social life and a school for Jewish children.

Teachers of the Law Men who in New Testament times taught and interpreted the teachings of the Old Testament, especially the first five books.

Tenant A person who grows crops on land owned by someone else, and turns over a part of the harvest to the owner to pay for the use of that land.

Topaz A semiprecious stone, usually yellow in color.

Turquoise A semiprecious stone, blue or bluish green in color.

Unleavened Bread, Festival of The Israelite festival, lasting seven days after Passover; it also celebrated the deliverance of the ancient Hebrews from Egypt. The name came from the practice of not using leaven (yeast) in making the bread during that week (Exodus 12.14-20). It was held from the 15th to the 22nd day of the month Nisan (around the first week of April).

Vow A strong declaration or promise, usually made while calling upon God to punish the speaker if the statement should prove to be not true or if the promise were not kept.

Winged creatures (also referred to as "living creatures" and traditionally called "cherubim") Symbol of God's majesty and associated with his presence. For a description of such creatures see Exodus 25.18-20; Ezekiel 1.5-13; Revelation 4.6-9.

Winnowing shovel A tool like a shovel or a large fork, used to separate the wheat from the chaff.

Wreath Flowers or leaves arranged in a circle, to be placed on a person's head. In ancient times a wreath of leaves was the prize given to winners in athletic contests.

Yeast A substance, also called leaven, which is added to dough made from the flour of wheat or barley to make it rise before being baked into bread.

Yoke A heavy bar of wood fitted over the necks of two oxen to make it possible for them to pull a plow or a cart. The word is used figuratively to describe the moral lessons that a teacher passes on to pupils.

Zeus The name of the supreme god of the Greeks.

Zion Originally a designation for "David's City," the Jebusite stronghold captured by King David's forces. The term "Zion" was later extended in meaning to refer to the hill on which the Temple stood.

Antioch
PISIDIA
Iconium
Lystra
Derbe
CILICIA
Tarsus
PAMPHYLIA
Attalia
Perga
LYCIA
Patara
Myra
Antioch
Seleucia
SYRIA
CYPRUS
Salamis
Paphos
Euphrates R.
MEDITERRANEAN
SEA
PHOENICIA
Sidon
Tyre
Damascus
Ptolemais
PALESTINE AND SYRIA
Caesarea
Samaria
0   Miles   200
Joppa
Lydda
0   Kms   200
Azotus
Jerusalem
Gaza
JUDEA
Alexandria

© United Bible Societies, 1976

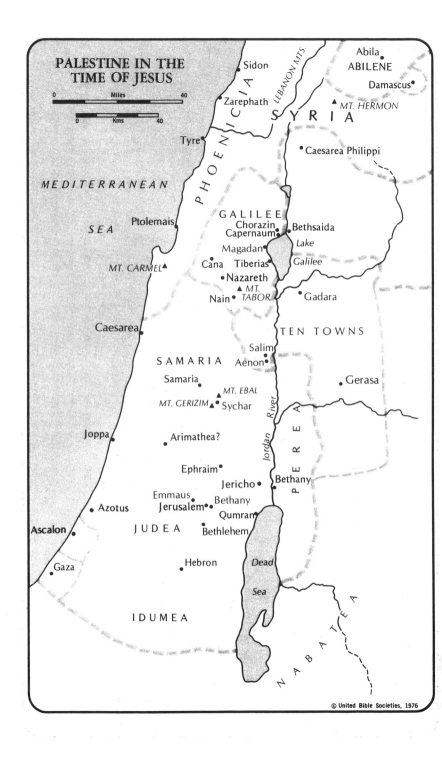

PALESTINE IN THE
TIME OF JESUS

Miles
0   40

Kms
0   40

Abila
ABILENE
Damascus

Sidon

Zarephath

LEBANON MTS.

SYRIA

▲ MT. HERMON

Tyre

PHOENICIA

• Caesarea Philippi

MEDITERRANEAN

SEA

Ptolemais

GALILEE

Chorazin
Capernaum • Bethsaida
Magadan   Lake
Cana Tiberias   Galilee
• Nazareth
▲ MT.
Nain • TABOR

MT. CARMEL ▲

Caesarea

• Gadara

TEN TOWNS

Salim •
Aenon •

SAMARIA

Samaria •

• Gerasa

MT. EBAL ▲
MT. GERIZIM ▲ • Sychar

Jordan River

P E R E A

Joppa

Arimathea? •

Ephraim •

Emmaus •   Jericho •   Bethany
Jerusalem • • Bethany
Azotus •   Qumran •

Ascalon •

JUDEA

Bethlehem •

• Hebron   Dead

Gaza •

Sea

IDUMEA

N A B A T E A

© United Bible Societies, 1976

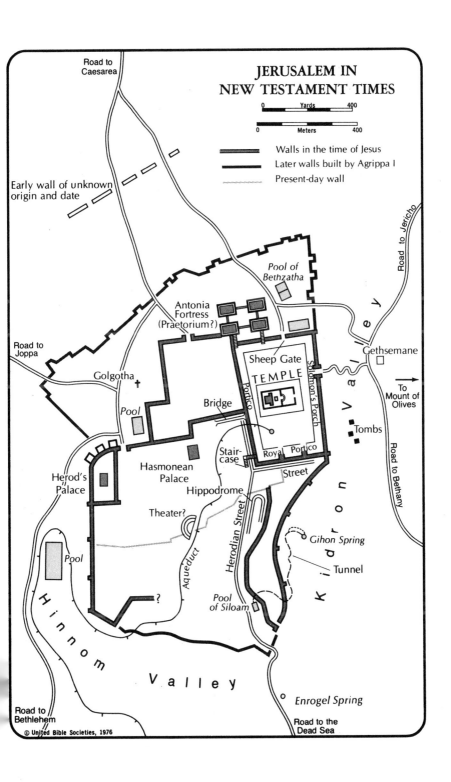

JERUSALEM IN
NEW TESTAMENT TIMES

Walls in the time of Jesus
Later walls built by Agrippa I
Present-day wall

Road to Caesarea

Early wall of unknown origin and date

Road to Jericho

Pool of Bethzatha

Antonia Fortress (Praetorium?)

Sheep Gate

Road to Joppa

Golgotha

TEMPLE

Gethsemane

To Mount of Olives

Portico

Solomon's Porch

Pool

Bridge

Tombs

Staircase

Royal Portico

Hasmonean Palace

Street

Herod's Palace

Hippodrome

Theater?

Gihon Spring

Aqueduct

Herodian Street

Tunnel

Kidron Valley

Pool

?

Pool of Siloam

H i n n o m   V a l l e y

Enrogel Spring

Road to Bethlehem

Road to the Dead Sea

© United Bible Societies, 1976